Overeducated and Over Here:
Skilled EU migrants in Britain

TRANSNATIONAL PRESS LONDON

Books by TPL

Overeducated and Over Here

Politics and Law in Turkish Migration

Family and Human Capital in Turkish Migration

Göç ve Uyum

Turkish Migration, Identity and Integration

Little Turkey in Great Britain (forthcoming)

Journals by TPL

Migration Letters

Remittances Review

Göç Dergisi

Journal of Gypsy Studies

Kurdish Studies

International Economics Letters

Border Crossing

Transnational Marketing Journal

Overeducated and Over Here: Skilled EU migrants in Britain

Bradley Saunders

TRANSNATIONAL PRESS LONDON
2015

OVEREDUCATED AND OVER HERE: SKILLED EU MIGRANTS IN BRITAIN

Bradley Saunders

Copyright © 2015 by Transnational Press London

First Published in 2015 by TRANSNATIONAL PRESS LONDON in the Ukinted Kingdom, 12 Ridgeway Gardens, London, N6 5XR, UK. www.tplondon.com

Transnational Press London® and the logo and its affiliated brands are registered trademarks.

Paperback

ISBN: 978-1-910781-04-3 ISBN: 978-1-80135-007-5 [Int. Edition]

Cover Photo: Altay Manço

Contents

Acknowledgements

This book is based on the doctoral thesis titled "Overeducated and Over Here – the Experiences of Skilled EU Migrants on Self-Initiated Foreign Work Experiences in Unskilled UK Jobs" submitted to Loughborough University, UK. An edited extract of this dissertation appeared as a book chapter titled "Opportunities and challenges for organisations and highly skilled migrant professionals" in Al Ariss, A. (ed.) (2014). *Global Talent Management, Challenges, Strategies, and Opportunities* (Springer, 2014). (co-authored by M. Nieto), pp.107-119.

This book would not be possible without the support of many people in Loughborough and elsewhere. My thanks go out to them all.

I would like to dedicate this book to all those who leave their homelands to seek work in foreign countries. I hope it helps others to better understand the motivations that drive them and the challenges they face.

About the author

Bradley Saunders received his PhD from Loughborough University (UK). Dr Saunders is Assistant Professor at Prince Mohammad Bin Fahd University, Saudi Arabia. He previously worked at University of Derby Online and Regent's University London in the UK. Bradley Saunders' teaching interests include International Management, Labour Relations, and Globalisation while his research mainly focuses on overeducation and underemployment among EU migrant workers, self-initiated expatriates, job transitions, and corporate expatriation and repatriation.

Introduction

As Denzin (1989:4) points out, one's choice of a topic to study and research is a "highly personal decision". Having spent approximately half my life away from my home country, it is perhaps not surprising that I chose to examine the lives of others who made similar decisions. As Cohen and Sirkeci (2011) argue, a culture of migration runs in the family too. As my father had immigrated to the UK from Poland and my wife was born overseas, I have myself been subjected, albeit unconsciously, to many years of outsiders' perspectives on the UK.

I have met many others who also left their home country's shores. Whether these were academics from London or labourers from Lahore, my conversations with them made me reflect on and question our life choices and experiences. Why had we decided to leave one country and move to another? Was there something different about us compared to our peers who did not make such a move? How did we view the experiences that resulted as a consequence of that decision?

Shortly before reaching the decision to repatriate to the UK from the Middle East in order to study for my PhD full time, I read Monica Ali's *Brick Lane* and was impressed by the mismatch between the pre-migration expectation and post-migration reality expressed by one of the characters:

I'm forty years old,' said Chanu. He spoke quietly like the doctor, with none of his assurance. 'I have been in this country for sixteen years. Nearly half my life. 'He gave a dry-throated gargle. "When I came I was a young man. I had ambitions. Big dreams. When I got off the aeroplane I had my degree certificate in my suitcase and a few pounds in my pocket. I thought there would be a red carpet laid out for me. I was going to join the Civil Service and become Private Secretary to the Prime Minister.' As he told his story, his voice grew. It filled the room. 'That was my plan. And then I found things were a bit different. These people here didn't know the difference between me, who stepped off an aeroplane with a degree certificate, and the peasants who jumped off the boat possessing only the lice on their heads. What can you do?' He rolled a ball of rice and meat in his fingers and teased it around his plate.

'I did this and that. Whatever I could. So much hard work, so little reward. More or less it is true to say I have been chasing wild buffaloes and eating my own rice. You know that saying? All the begging letters from home I

1

burned. And I made two promises to myself. I will be a success, come what may. That's promise number one. Number two, I will go back home. When I am a success. And I will honour these promises.' Chanu, who had grown taller and taller in his chair, sank back down.
   'Very good, very good,' said Dr Azad. He checked his watch.
Monica Ali, (2003) Brick Lane, p.34

These words added an extra dimension to my prior interest in expatriation, such as my Masters dissertation on expatriate academics in Dubai, namely that of an inability to find work commensurate with one's abilities and qualifications. Little in what I had previously read addressed this issue, as the expatriation literature in which I had been submerged seemed to assume that any expatriation would be to a post at the same or a higher level than that previously held. I began to sense that the plight of those who settled for less in their pursuit of more would be too interesting to ignore. This book is the result of that interest.

On 1st May 2004, millions of citizens from eight former Soviet bloc countries (Czech Republic, Estonia, Hungary, Latvia, Lithuania, Poland, Slovakia and Slovenia - henceforth A8) gained the right of freedom of movement in the European Union. This freedom of movement, however, did not automatically confer the right to work throughout the community. Twelve of the fifteen existing Member States had imposed temporary restrictions on the right of A8 migrants to work. The exceptions were Ireland, Sweden, and the United Kingdom (UK).

The UK's offer of immediate free access to A8 workers resulted in a larger-than-expected influx of A8 migrants to the UK, which caused a public backlash and heated debates over the benefits and costs of large-scale immigration. Much has been written about the political and economic impact of this influx. This book focusses instead on the complex interweaving factors affecting the work and nonwork lives of skilled migrant workers in the UK working in jobs which are not commensurate with their work experience, skills and interests. The focus on the European context addresses the need for a better understanding of contemporary labour mobility within the EU (Khapova, Vinkenburg & Arnold, 2009; Mayrhofer & Schneidhofer, 2009).

The important, though often neglected, perspective of individuals who take on work below their level (Arnold & Cohen, 2008) forms the focus of this book. In-depth interviews analyse the lived experiences of migrant workers in the UK working in jobs which are not commensurate with their qualifications and experience. The aim is to gain an insight into the migrant workers' reasons for coming; the barriers they faced in their search for employment commensurate with their qualifications and experience; and their adjustment to their new work, cultural and social environments.

Migrant workers who have come of their own volition to the United Kingdom either to take up a post or to look for a job often take on work which is not commensurate with their educational qualifications and experience. This places them in a situation of overeducation, or skill- and status-underemployment. By investigating the mismatch between migrants' prior education and home country experience and the type of employment which they obtain in the UK, this book aims to contribute to the growing interest (Drinkwater, Eade, & Garapich, 2006; Johnston et al., 2010; Khattab et al., 2011; Felker, 2011; Sirkeci et al., 2014) in the experiences of the migrant workforce in the UK.

In this study answers to four questions are sought: The first of these draws on research in the field of geographical mobility and aims to arrive at an understanding of the factors that have led to their decision to come to the United Kingdom in search of work: What are the factors that influence the migrant workers' decision to come to the UK to take up or seek work? Then, questions about career transition, expatriate adjustment and overeducation and underemployment emerge: What barriers do these migrants face in finding work commensurate with their qualifications and experience? How do they cope with the skill- and status- underemployment in the jobs they take on? How do nonwork and family factors affect their adjustment to living and working in the UK? The answers to these four questions and the insights they bring should provide us with a better understanding of the career transition experiences of migrant workers.

A qualitative approach was taken in order to find these answers. Most research in this field is dominated by quantitative approaches (Singleton, 1999; Robinson and Carey, 2000) despite a recent surge in qualitative studies (e.g. Trevena, 2008; Anderson et al, 2006; Eade, Drinkwater, & Garapich, 2007). To allow for personal experiences, aspirations, feelings and responses (De Tona, 2006), a qualitative enquiry is chosen as appropriate in this study in the hope of gaining an insight into the phenomenon of skilled migrants working in unskilled jobs from the perspective of the migrants themselves. This study is based in the constructivist paradigm and adopts an interpretivist epistemology. This means that the way in which phenomena are investigated and the meaning of the findings of such investigations are dependent on the context in which the investigations take place. Findings here cannot therefore be generalised but can be expected to be relevant to audiences which relate to that context.

Being aware that a large number of recent studies (e.g. Currie, 2006; Drinkwater, Eade & Garapich, 2006; Trevena, 2010) focussed on Polish migrants, the largest immigrant workers group in the UK (Dickinson et al,

2008), I was at first tempted to restrict the study to Polish nationals but went for a wider variety. A purposive or judgement sample was selected to allow me to interview individuals whose backgrounds and experience were such as to provide useful insights. Participants were also expected to have a good command of spoken English so that I could interview them. A snowball method was used to select participants. Of the 19 interviewees, 11 were female and eight male. Nine were Polish, three Brazilian, two Latvian, two Lithuanian, one French, one Iranian and one Portuguese (The non-EU migrants also held a second passport from an EU country).

Semi-structured in-depth interviews, the most commonly used data collection method in this type of research, were chosen to generate rich data. It is a well understood method which "...has its natural basis in human conversation" (Hannabuss, 1996:22). The main focus was to encourage migrant workers to talk about their experiences of living and working in the UK. Finally, the length of the interviews ranged from 40 minutes to two and a quarter hours. These were conducted at homes, work places and cafes and participants were informed of the details and consent was sought through a consent form to be completed by the respondents. No participant is identified by name and care has been taken to present information so that individuals are not identifiable.

The fully transcribed interviews were then analysed using HyperRESEARCH, a software that aids with the coding of text and multimedia, the retrieval of coded text and grouping of coded segments, the statistical analysis of frequency of code occurrence, the testing of propositions by use of Boolean searches on a code or codes, and the testing of hypotheses through the use of artificial intelligence (Smith & Hesse-Biber, 1996). Once I had my list of codes (reduced from around 800 to around 200) I needed to be able to order and interrelate them, so that, for example the disparate list of codes above - 'came because needed money', 'came to visit sister', 'came to study', 'came for children's education' - could be regrouped into a major theme "Reasons for Coming" and a number of sub themes such as 'financial', 'family', 'education' and so on. After the coding process, I used a CAQDAS program for mindmapping. Coding in HyperRESEARCH and organising the codes in ConceptDraw Mindmap worked well. It enabled me to avoid a further danger that of treating the map as an independent means of analysis and ignoring or forgetting the relationship of the visual representation to the original verbal text (Butler-Kisber & Poldma, 2009) since HyperRESEARCH made it easy to retrieve the codes in their original context. Hence the narratives you will read in this book are drawn from the transciptions of the interviews.

Chapter 1: Clarifying the terminology

When I use a word,' Humpty Dumpty said, in a rather scornful tone,' it means just what I choose it to mean, neither more nor less.'
'The question is,' said Alice, 'whether you can make words mean so many different things.'
'The question is,' said Humpty Dumpty, 'which is to be master - that's all.'

Lewis Carroll: Through the Looking Glass

Migrants, migrant workers and self-initiated expatriates

In order to avoid any lack of clarity in terminology, it is important for us to compare the way the terms "migrant", "migrant worker" and "self-initiated expatriate" are used within the literature on international careers and the wider mobility literature.

Green, Owen & Wilson (2005) bemoan the lack of clarity of the terms 'migrant' and 'migrant worker'. Indeed, Bell, Jarman & Lefebvre (2004:11) argue that "A precise or universally agreed definition of the term 'migrant worker' does not exist" and highlight disparities in various definitions from the United Nations, the International Labour Organisation, the Labour Force Survey and the International Passenger Survey (IPS).

One very broad definition is "someone who has entered the UK with the intention to work" (Schneider and Holman, 2005:7), which is closely matched by "individuals who arrive in the host country with the intention of finding a job" (Zaronaite and Tirzite, 2005:7). The core concept of arriving in a host country to find a job is gradually refined in other definitions with the Commission for Rural Communities (2007) distinguishing between the intention to work and the existence of a job agreed to before departure: "an individual who arrives in the host country either with a job to go to or with the intention of finding one" (CRC, 2007: 4).

A further refinement is provided by the International Passenger Survey (IPS) - often cited in official reports as the source of immigration data - which stipulates the length of time the migrant worker intends to spend in the UK by defining a migrant worker as 'a person who has resided abroad for a year or more, and who states on arrival the intention to stay in the UK for a year or more'. This definition would seem to exclude seasonal workers (McKay & Winkelmann-Gleed, 2005) and others on short term contracts.

Whereas some (e.g. McKay & Winkelmann-Gleed, 2005), argue that irregular migrants, whose stay remains undocumented, should fall within this definition, others (e.g. De Lima, Jentsch, & Whelton, 2005) implicitly rule out the latter group by requiring proof of the right to work, such as a National Insurance number. However, the stipulation that a National Insurance number has been issued would appear to exclude those migrants who have arrived in search of work until such time as they take it up, which does not seem very productive.

Suutari and Brewster (2000) identified the need for more research into the increasing number of self-initiated expatriates (SIEs) travelling abroad to find work. Lee (2005:173) defined an SIE as "any individual who is hired as an individual on contractual basis and not transferred overseas by parent organizations".

Despite the overriding focus in the expatriation literature being placed predominantly on company managers being sent overseas, largely to a subsidiary, for set periods of time, SIEs form a much larger proportion of those working abroad than those who are sent abroad by their Multinational Corporation employers (Bonache, Brewster, & Suutari, 2001; Carr, Inkson, & Thorn, 2005; Inkson et al, 1997; Lee, 2005). This focus in the literature on expatriate assignees leaves a gap in our understanding of those who independently seek work abroad (Bonache Brewster & Suutari, 2001; Richardson, 2003; Scott, 2006).

Suutari and Brewster (2000) surveyed 448 Finnish graduate engineers working outside of Finland. They found that a sizeable proportion of the respondents (147 or 33%) were on self-initiated work assignments. They identified several key characteristics - demographic factors such as more females, more working couples and more singles; the lack of planning for repatriation, and a variety of salary levels which were generally lower than those of traditional expatriates. Their categorisation of self-initiated expatriates (SIEs) into six groups - young opportunists, localised professionals, job seekers, international professionals, officials and dual-career couples - helped to expand the category of SIEs to include not just young people at an early stage in their careers but more experienced individuals.

Bonache, Brewster & Suutari (2001) also stress the diversity of the backgrounds of SIEs, citing self-initiated foreign assignments and overseas postings in non-commercial international aid organisations and charities as two areas in which individuals independently decide to take up foreign postings outside of an organisational setting.

Richardson (2003) expanded the scope of SIEs even further by focussing on the experiences of 30 British expatriate academics in New Zealand, Singapore, Turkey and the United Arab Emirates, who had expatriated independently. In so doing, she established expatriate academics as a subset of SIEs. Froese (2011) further developed Richardson's (2003) work by examining a more diverse sample of self-initiated expatriate academics living and working in Korea.

Felker (2011) identifies a further group as SIEs, namely young, well-educated Eastern Europeans seeking career development in Western Europe. In so doing, she blurs the boundaries between two groups – SIEs and migrants (or migrant workers) which are conceptually very similar and yet are typically researched in different literatures. In this she is not alone. For example, Carr, Inkson & Thorn (2005:387) refer to "migrants who expatriate themselves voluntarily to new countries independently of any employer".

As part of a study examining the experiences of Lebanese migrants in France, Al Ariss (2010) compares the use of the terms 'migrant' and 'SIE' within the international career literature, noting that the latter term is of more recent origin than the former. He differentiates them based on four criteria:

1. the geographical origin and destination of the move
2. the degree of voluntariness of the move
3. the length of stay in the destination country
4. the status conferred on the groups in the destination country

Al Ariss' classification of the two groups is summarised in Table 1:

Table 1. Migrants vs. SIEs (based on Al Ariss, 2010)

	Migrants	**SIEs**
Origin	Developing countries	Developed countries
Voluntariness	Need to move	Choose to move
Length of Stay	Permanent	Temporary
Status	Looked on unfavourably	Seen in a positive light

Despite these distinctions, Al Ariss (2010) acknowledges that, in practice, use of the two terms is inconsistent, pointing out several instances which contradict each of the above categories. Extending his analysis of the use of the two terms in the literature on international careers to the wider mobility literature sheds some light on the distinctions he makes.

Firstly, as Al Ariss concedes, many studies in the literature on international careers do not differentiate between migrants and SIEs based on their country of origin. Within the wider mobility literature however, a distinction emerges between migrants from within and without the EU. Dench et al (2006) point out the differences in the freedom of movement and eligibility to work of migrant workers in the UK from a) the 14 older European Union states, b) the eight new Accession states; and c) non-EU countries. The EU nation states have generally encouraged EU citizens to move between EU countries and discouraged non-EU citizens from entering the EU (Penninx, Spencer & Hear, 2008). In the UK, not only the Coalition Government (2010-15) but also its Labour predecessor and Conservative successor have implemented steps to reduce both unskilled and skilled immigration from outside of the EU.

Members of other EU states – who accounted for almost half of the 2008 influx into the UK (The Economist, 18th November, 2010) continue, however, to have free access into the country. This produces a situation in which a highly skilled non-EU citizen may be unable to enter the country or have his or her employment tightly regulated, whilst his or her EU counterpart can enter without let or hindrance, even without a job offer in the pipeline. The question of freedom of movement enjoyed by EU citizens, absent from the literature on SIEs, is important for the purpose of this study, since it plays an important role in the theoretical background.

Secondly, a distinction on the basis of voluntariness is not entirely clear cut, since the ability to choose to do or to refuse to do something is often constrained by circumstances (Ashforth, 2001). Thus a migrant may move to the UK because he or she would otherwise be unable to buy food or rent shelter. Similarly, an SIE may choose to visit the UK to try and find work after being made redundant at home. To what extent these can then be said to be voluntary acts is open to question.

The contrast between voluntariness and involuntariness lies in the extent of the individual's sense of control. If we adopt the description of involuntary transitions as those brought about by "influential others or uncontrollable forces" (Ashforth, 2001:111), a clear distinction emerges between individuals leaving their home country as a result of war and political instability, such as the Lebanese in Al Ariss' (2010) study, and European "free movers" (Favell, 2008) choosing to exercise their freedom of movement throughout the EU to seek work in another member state.

Thirdly, although individuals who have fled their home countries as the result of forced migration may not contemplate return, Al Ariss (2010) concedes that several studies identify an open-endedness in the international movements of SIEs. This lack of planning can lead to SIEs staying on indefinitely and thus becoming indistinguishable from migrants in this respect. For EU nationals, the absence of any visa requirements may persuade them to stay on in the UK for longer than originally planned (McKay & Winkelmann-Gleed, 2005). Conversely, as a direct result of the freedom of movement they enjoy, those initially expressing the intention to stay for a longer term may in fact decide to leave early, or may leave with the intention of remaining in their home country but then return to the UK after a short period of time. Indeed, within Europe:

"... most migration is not permanent, but part of a process of mobility in which both return and serial migration are natural economic responses to a dynamic economy" (Piracha & Vickerman, 2002:1).

Thus, the criterion of permanency of stay is difficult to apply to the individuals in this study.

Fourthly, the term "migrant" carries some negative connotations which are absent in the literature on SIEs (Al Ariss, 2010; Cohen and Sirkeci, 2011). They are "... poor, uprooted, marginal and desperate" (King, 2002:89), hybrids and bad social products who "blur the borders of the national order" (Sayad, 2004:291), and "welfare-scroungers, job-snatchers and threats to stability" (The Economist, 4th May, 2000). These are clearly not terms by which free-moving EU citizens, whom Favell (2008) refers to as 'eurostars', would wish to be described.

Participants in Al Ariss' (2010) study complained of discrimination on the basis of "traits such as language, religion, and manners of dress" (p. 348). Such racist undercurrents are largely absent from the few studies of SIEs to date, yet quite frequent in discussions in the wider mobility literature of migrant workers in the UK. For example, Bell, Jarman & Lefebvre (2004) found that migrant workers in Northern Ireland, despite being white, still displayed enough visible differences (e.g. language) to be shunned by the local populace as "other". Eade, Drinkwater & Garapich (2006:17-18) found that Polish migrant workers in the UK emphasised their race over their nationality since being "white, European and Christian" helped them to disassociate themselves from "the wrong social class" and identify themselves with "the dominant white English group".

Since the SIE literature is still in its infancy (Felker, 2011), discussion of negative perceptions of SIEs by the local populace is still largely absent from the literature on international careers. However, to distinguish between migrants and SIEs on the basis of how they are perceived by the indigenous population may not accurately distinguish between the two groups but rather simply reflect the fact that those individuals referred to as migrant workers in the wider mobility literature possess more visibly distinguishing features than those referred to as SIEs in the literature on international careers.

Glanz, Williams & Hoeksema (2001) suggest that in order to reflect the role individuals play in actively pursuing their career interests, current definitions of expatriates as employees who are assigned temporarily overseas should be replaced with a definition such as 'people and families who move internationally in pursuit of their occupation' (Glanz, Williams & Hoeksema, 2001:102). This distinction is an important one, as individual issues must be understood in order to reflect the changing reality of expatriates and expatriation.

Skill

One essential characteristic for the individuals in this study, which is implicitly but not explicitly addressed in the discussions of SIEs and migrants referred to above, is the notion of being skilled. Scott (2006) acknowledges the importance of this dimension when critiquing the organisational perspective within accounts of skilled migration, identifying the failure of the professional expatriate model alone to explain the phenomenon of skilled migration.

Since the term 'skilled' is widely used in migration research, it seemed appropriate to refer to 'skilled migrants' in the current study. However, the meaning of the term 'skill' is problematical. Noon and Blyton (1997: 78) observe that "skill is a definitional minefield". Korczynski (2005:4) claims that it has been misused so much "that it risks coming to mean everything yet nothing." Several alternatives to the term 'skilled migrants' have been put forward including 'professional transients' (Appleyard, 1989) and 'the migration of expertise' (Salt & Singleton, 1995).

The holding of a degree or extensive specialised work experience has frequently been employed as a common yardstick in studies of skilled migrants (Dumont & Lemaitre, 2005; Iredale, 2001; Salt, 1997; Vertovec, 2002). However, this appears an arbitrary and vague measure (Koser & Salt, 1997). Surely the skill possessed by highly trained craftsmen such as builders, plumbers or carpenters is more, not less, valuable to an employer than the skills of the holder of an Arts degree (Mahroum, 2000; Skeldon, 2005)? After all, the popular press in the UK placed more emphasis on the challenges to UK workers posed by Polish plumbers than those posed by Polish History graduates. Perhaps, then, as the Global Commission on International Migration (GCIM, 2005) suggest in a 2005 report, the emphasis on educational levels is misplaced, since non-academically skilled workers such as carers are as essential as those with tertiary qualifications.

The nature of the skills of the migrant workers in this study varies in several respects. Not all of them have tertiary qualifications. Some hold specialised technical and vocational diplomas. Their skills are not exclusively of an academic nature. Nor do they need to be. All of the migrants in this study possess a skill, or a set of skills, distinguishing them from unskilled workers. Yet they were working in unskilled jobs at the time that the study was conducted.

Categorising migrants

Several researchers have developed typologies based on the strategies adopted by migrants. A typology created by Drinkwater, Eade & Garapich (2006), differentiates between groups of Polish migrants based on their migration strategy, settlement plans and the extent of their engagement in transnational activities. It distinguishes between *Storks* (seasonal migrants), *Hamsters* (one-off migrants seeking to build up investment capital), *Searchers* (uncommitted and ambitious migrants with a transnational outlook) and *Stayers* (long-term migrants with little, if any, intention of leaving).

Similarly, Duvell and Vogel (2006) categorise migrants based on their intentions. Within the broad category of *return-oriented migrants*, are those who arrive to learn, to travel or to acquire capital before heading home. In contrast, *emigrants/immigrants* decide to settle, through lifestyle choice or marriage, whilst *transnational migrants* carry out a dual existence between their homeland and the country of destination. *Global nomads*, on the other hand, like Drinkwater, Eade, & Garapich's (2006) *Searchers*, do not restrict themselves to one destination country, but constantly seek out new opportunities wherever these might present themselves.

Trevena (2006) also presents a typology of migrants based on their plans for professional mobility and differentiates between *rational career planners*, who are determined to work hard in order to achieve success; *escapists*, who are more interested in nonwork activities in the UK than in their work; and *temporary workers*, who plan to return to Poland where they will put the capital they gain during their stay in the UK to use.

The utility of such typologies is, however, questioned as such groupings are ideal categories into which actual migrants may not necessarily fit. The interviewees in this book often started out in one category, but then their plans changed. For example, some started out with the definite intention of returning after three months but decided to stay on, having found a job which was more lucrative, or having met someone with whom they wanted to enter into a long-term romantic relationship.

Intercultural adjustment

As individuals and their families move across national boundaries, they encounter cultural differences to those prevalent in the societies in which they grew up, differences for which they are often unprepared. (Hofstede, 2001). An inability to adjust to such differences can lead to such problems as substance abuse, workaholism, psychological terror, mental health problems, confusion over one's identity, and dissatisfaction (Webb and Wright, 1996; Grinstein & Wathieu, 2008). An appreciation, then, of how cultures differ and how individuals overcome the challenge of adaptation to a new culture is of relevance to an understanding of the experiences of the migrants in this study.

The growth in the number of international assignments over the last few decades has increased awareness of international adjustment (Andreason, 2008; Aycan, 1997, Bhaskar-Shrinivas et al., 2005; Grinstein & Wathieu, 2008; Shay & Baack; Van Vianen et al., 2004) or degree of fit and psychological comfort and familiarity that individuals feel towards different aspects of a foreign culture and the concomitant reduction of conflict (Berry, 1992).

Berry (1997) proposed a framework in which immigrants' attitudes towards acculturation are identified in terms of their choices to two basic options:

1 to maintain their cultural identity and characteristics
OR
2 to reject their cultural identity and characteristics
AND
3 to maintain relationships with the dominant society
OR
4 to reject relationships with the dominant society

These two choices result in an acculturation strategy of:
1 + 3 = integration
2 + 3 = assimilation
1 + 4 = separation: segregation
2 + 4 = marginalisation

Studies (Schmitz, 1995; Berry, 1997; van Oudenhoven and Eisses, 1998) have identified integration and assimilation as the preferred strategies of the majority of immigrants, whereas Berry et al (1987) and Ward and Kennedy (1994) identified a link between the choice of strategy and the level of acculturation stress. Zimmermann, Holman & Sparrow (2003) review several other attempts to investigate these modes of adjustment to intercultural interactions, including that of Janssens (1995). Other similar acculturation models have been proposed (Phinney, 1990; Bourhis et al., 1997).

Such bi-dimensional acculturation models appear to be based on the assumption that immigrants can freely choose an acculturation strategy

(Kosic, 2002). However, as Berry (1997) explains, the choice of a strategy may be affected by the broader national context. Migrants are not free to choose a strategy if the dominant society's attitude to cultural diversity is neither open nor inclusive. To this end, national policies and programmes may also need to be analysed in terms of the four strategies (Berry, 1992).

Many A8 migrants appear to be rejecting relationships with British people. Spencer et al (2007:58) found that even after two years in the UK, "…one in four [migrants] still say that they spent no leisure time at all with British people". This they ascribed to the aloofness of the British as well as to lack of language ability. Inability to communicate effectively in English was not only a cause, but in many cases a result, of this lack of contact. In addition to these factors, Trevena (2009) points out the cultural and educational differences between migrants and their British co-workers and argues that:

> *"apart from sharing similar job responsibilities and/or living in the same area, the better-educated Poles generally have little in common with their British co-workers and neighbours" (Trevena, 2009:21).*

Trevena's study, like many others (e.g. Currie, 2006; 2007; Drinkwater, Eade & Garapich, 2006) was restricted to Poles in the UK. As the largest group by far among new European arrivals (Robinson, 2002; Audit Commission, 2007), Polish migrants dominate the job market. Cook, Dwyer & Waite (2011) report on the animosity felt towards Polish migrants by Slovak and Roma migrants who resented the existence of specialist Polish recruitment agencies and the support network of established Polish communities dating from the post-WWII wave of Polish migrants. This sectarianism suggests that A8 migrants might not just lack contact with British people but also with migrants from different countries. Thus a picture emerges of highly-educated migrants lacking contact with educated locals, lacking empathy with uneducated locals, and resenting, or being resented by, other educated migrants from neighbouring countries.

A8 migrants with qualifications and skills in excess of that required by their jobs often compete for jobs, not with UK or EU nationals, but with members of ethnic minorities. For many of them, this is both a surprise and a source of friction and they express "… strongly negative views towards Asian people in particular" (Spencer et al., 2007:71).

The growth in short term and circular migration in recent years (Peltonen, 2001), has made it easier for migrant workers to avoid an integration or assimilation strategy and to lessen the acculturation stress associated with the other two strategies. Maintaining one's cultural identity is easier when new communication opportunities such as the Internet, mobile phones and e-mail have brought 'home' closer and allowed migrants to:

"... carry their imagined communities with them to an even greater degree than before and actively use these in constructing and maintaining their identities despite spatial dispersion." *(Madsen and van Naerssen, 2003:68)*

Migrants may also make frequent trips home – Eade, Drinkwater & Garapich (2007) report that 4 in 5 of their interviewees made trips home to Poland several times a year.

The international aspect of transitions brings with it an added layer of complexity insofar as the need to come to terms with new work-related changes is supplemented by the need to adjust to general differences outside of work. Takeuchi (2010) highlights the effect that adjustment has on family members and other stakeholders such as host country and parent country nationals.

In "... the most influential and often-cited theoretical treatment of expatriate experiences" (Bhaskar-Shrinivas et al., 2005:257), Black, Mendenhall and Oddou (1991) highlight the importance of non-work factors in the expatriate adjustment process, stressing that moving:

" ... to a foreign country often involves changes in the job the individual performs and the corporate culture in which responsibilities are executed; it can also involve dealing with unfamiliar norms related to the general culture, business practices, living conditions, weather, food, health care, daily customs, and political systems - plus facing a foreign language on a daily basis." (Black, Mendenhall and Oddou, 1991:292)

Black, Mendenhall and Oddou (1991) identified three related but conceptually distinct aspects of intercultural adjustment:

1. *work adjustment, involving the adaptation to new job tasks, work roles, and the new work environment;*
2. *interaction adjustment, or the comfort achieved in interacting with Host Country Nationals in both work and non-work situations;*
3. *general adjustment to non-work activities which comprises factors affecting daily life in the new setting such as living and housing conditions, food, health care, and cost of living.*

This typology has been adopted by several researchers (Selmer, 1998, Van Vianen et al., 2004, Palthe, 2004). The dimensions are also similar to those of psychological adjustment, socio-cultural adjustment and work adjustment used by Aycan (1997) in her study of acculturation among expatriate managers.

A great deal of emphasis has been placed on adjustment within a work context, often focusing on the demands placed on expatriates when communicating and interacting with local employees (Black, 1988; Van Vianen et al., 2004; Peltokorpi, 2007). Whilst such adjustment is necessary for all those transitioning to a new context in a foreign setting, it is reasonable to expect that individuals transferring to an overseas branch of their own company will face fewer demands in terms of work adaptation than individuals on self-initiated assignments joining a foreign-run company, who in turn will face fewer adjustment demands than those travelling abroad independently to take up work in an entirely different field or profession. It is this latter group which is of interest in the present study.

Despite the attention to work adjustment in the expatriation literature, far less attention has been given to nonwork or general lifestyle adjustment practices in the host country (Grinstein & Wathieu, 2008; Andreason, 2008). Aycan (1997) highlights the importance to successful expatriate adjustment of expatriates' being willing to communicate with host nationals. She further points out the danger of restricting one's interactions to the 'expatriate ghetto' and so failing to gain familiarity with and understanding of nationals of the country to which one has relocated.

Takeuchi, Yun and Russell (2002) stress the importance of language proficiency in successful interaction adjustment, pointing out the importance of a good command of the host country language in order not only to exchange information, establish relationships and feel comfortable when interacting with nationals but also to gain an understanding of cultural idiosyncrasies which might be impossible to comprehend without such a command of the language. Green, Owen and Jones (2008) stress the importance of the need for migrants to overcome the barrier of poor English skills both inside and outside of the workplace.

A8 migrants arriving in the UK are faced with a new linguistic setting. Some may have arrived with little or no English. Others will have studied the language at school or even university but may well find that the English they hear spoken on the streets of London, in the strawberry fields in Lincolnshire, or by their Indian co-workers, is not the same as the English they studied. Especially for those with a lower level of English on arrival, the possibility of improving their command of the language without taking classes is low.

However, they may encounter obstacles to being able to attend English language classes. Migrants may face difficulties in enrolling on classes or keeping up a regular attendance because of the shift patterns that they work, frequent trips to their home country, or an inability to find free or affordable courses (Wales Rural Observatory, 2006; CRC, 2007). Spencer et al (2007) point out that those migrants who were able to overcome these barriers were not those whose need for such classes was the greatest.

Identity
Failure to adjust to one's new surroundings can lead to confusion over

one's identity. Trevena (2010) studied a group of highly educated Poles in menial jobs in London. Using Breakwell's Socio-Psychological Identity Model (Breakwell, 1983) and Bourdieu's Triad (Bourdieu & Wacquant, 1992), she examined participants' motives for migrating, the influence of their migration experience on identity and values, and the impact on their aspirations and future plans.

The jobs that people do can impact the perception of their identity to an equal or greater extent than their personal lives or factors such as race, gender, age, ethnicity, or nationality (Tracy & Trethewey 2005; Hochschild, 1997; Hogg & Terry, 2000). Hall (2002) claims that career identities play a significant part in self-perception insofar as asking "What do you do?" equates to asking "Who are you?" (Hall, 2002:170). It would follow then, that as a result of migrants leaving one career path behind and entering into menial jobs, they may notice a substantial change not only in the way that others see them but also in the way that they begin to see themselves.

Some of an individual's identities will be more prominent than others (McCall & Simmons, 1978). The prominence of a particular identity is dependent on factors such as support, commitment and reward (Stets & Burke, 2003). The centrality of a particular identity evolves with time in accordance with the different circumstances in which individuals find themselves (Denzin, 1992). Owens (2003) points out that individuals relate to these various role identities differently, with more prominent identities evoking a positive or "me-too" reaction, and less prominent ones evoking a negative or "not-me" reaction. McCall (2003) highlighted the need to research such "not-me" reactions, or self-disidentifications rather than restrict one's focus to self-identifications. This would suggest a need to concentrate on the 'I'm not a menial worker' reaction rather than the 'I'm actually a skilled and experienced IT specialist' reaction.

It is in the interaction between roles that meaning is created. Others respond to an individual as a result of their interactions with that individual in a specific role identity. The individual then reflexively constructs a sense of self-meaning and self-definition from these responses (Hogg & Terry, 2000). A gap between that self-concept and the ideal self will lead to a decrease in self esteem, which is exacerbated by real or imagined perceptions of our looking glass selves (Cooley, 1902) and by the effect of a low social status within society (Stets & Burke, 2003).

Two major concepts help us to understand the fact that many highly-skilled immigrants can find themselves in a situation of 'brain-waste' or 'brain abuse' (Bauder, 2003; Brandi, 2001; Koser & Salt, 1997) in which they are unable to escape from menial jobs. These are the interrelated concepts of overeducation and underemployment. It is necessary for us to examine these concepts, how they are related and how they impact the lives of the migrants in this study.

Overeducation

An individual is overeducated if his or her level of education exceeds that required for the performance of his or her job (Sloane, Battu, & Seaman, 1999; Linsley, 2005; Lianos, 2007; Felstead, Gallie, & Green, 2002). The incidence of overeducation can be determined in both a subjective and an objective fashion. The subjective determination of overeducation relies upon reports by the jobholders themselves in which they compare their educational level with that required for the job they are performing. A drawback of the subjective method is that it depends on respondents' perceptions and runs the risk that they may overstate job requirements or merely recite hiring practice standards (Kler, 2006). The objective determination of overeducation utilises job analysis data to establish the extent of mismatch between the level of education required by the job and that of the jobholder (Kler, 2006; Bishop, 1993).

Overeducation can be measured objectively by reference to either a national or international occupational classification. An example of the use of the former is Pemberton's (2008) study using the UK Government's Standard Occupational Classification (SOC) as a yardstick with which to compare the educational level of migrant workers in the North West of the UK with the skills needed in their jobs. This revealed that a large majority of those surveyed had held positions at a higher level before coming to the UK.

Similarly, in a Europe-wide analysis of occupational promotion of migrant workers, Barone (2009) illustrates how objective measurement of overeducation by means of a comparison between the International Standard Classification of Education (ISCED) and the International Standard Classification of Occupations (ISCO) schema was used to identify clear and widespread overeducation of migrant workers in the EU. This presented a picture of migrant workers with qualifications obtained outside of the destination country having a much higher incidence of overeducation than natives of that country. In other words, an objective measure of the gap between skills held and skills required in the current job revealed that migrant workers were much more likely than native workers to be working in a position below their education level.

Relative to employees with appropriate qualifications for the job, overeducated employees have been found to show lower productivity and job satisfaction (Tsang, Rumberger, & Levin, 1991) and to be more likely to seek a job change (Robst, 1995; Sicherman, 1991). The effects of overeducation can be especially marked if overeducation is experienced as a permanent, rather than a temporary phenomenon (Dolton & Vignoles, 2000; Battu & Sloane, 2002; Rubb, 2003).

Workers may temporarily accept jobs for which they are overqualified because of the costs involved in finding a more appropriate job (Johnson, 1978; Jovanovic, 1979). Entry-level jobs may offer employees the opportunity to gain experience, obtain on-the-job training and search for better career opportunities (Groot, 1996; Sicherman, 1991). If they are subsequently successful in obtaining such opportunities, then overeducation will have been a temporary experience for them.

Migrants may be more susceptible to overeducation than native-born labour market participants (Flatau, Petridis, & Wood, 1995; Chiswick & Miller, 2009). This is supported by studies in several countries – e.g. Greece (Lianos, 1997; Patrinos, 1997); Denmark (Nielsen, 2007, Liversage, 2009); Canada (Bauder, 2003); Australia (Kler, 2006; Green, Kler and Leeves, 2007) and the UK (Waddington, 2007; Battu & Sloane, 2002). A study conducted by the OECD (2006) in 21 countries also revealed a higher percentage of over-educated individuals among immigrant workers than among the native-born population. A 2013 report for the International Organization for Migration (IOM) pointed out widespread evidence of a clear underutilization of immigrants' skills throughout the EU (Schuster, Desiderio & Urso, 2013).

The above studies identified several factors causing the high rate of overeducation among immigrants, including:

- poor ability in the local language
- lack of local work experience
- non-recognition of academic qualifications
- lack of knowledge about how the labour market functions
- inability to enter regulated professions requiring membership of professional bodies
- insufficient financial resources to fund long job searches

These findings suggest that the pressure on migrants to find paid employment quickly, the difficulty and delay in having their qualifications recognised and the vicious circle of needing local experience in order to be given local experience may combine to make overeducation a long-term, rather than temporary, experience for highly-skilled migrants.

Underemployment

Differing definitions of the concept of underemployment exist. Indeed, Friedland and Price (2003:33) lament the fact that "… there are almost as many operational definitions of *underemployment* as there are researchers studying the phenomenon (italics in original). All of these definitions have two things in common, however - a view of underemployment as an inferior or lower quality type of employment and reference to a standard of comparison against which underemployment comes short (Feldman, 1996).

Underemployment is generally seen as an inadequacy along the dimensions of time, income and skill (Clogg, Eliason, & Wahl, 1990; Clogg, Sullivan, & Mutchler, 1986; Hauser, 1974; Sullivan, 1978). In addition, it can also reflect an inadequacy in social status (Burris, 1983; Friedland & Price, 2003). Here we examine each of these inadequacies in turn.

Time-related underemployment has been referred to as 'visible underemployment' in contrast with 'invisible underemployment'. This is because the former is quantifiable through counting the number of hours worked. In contrast, the latter is brought about by a misallocation of labour resources, under-utilisation of skill, and other hard-to-quantify factors (Brown & Pintaldi, 2006; Simic, 2002).

Time-related underemployment occurs when the hours of work of an employed person are below a threshold, and are insufficient in relation to "an alternative employment situation in which persons are willing and available to engage." (ILO, 1998). It affects individuals who are working fewer hours than they would prefer to work and who are willing to work additional hours, in any of the following ways:

- by taking on another job in addition to their current job(s)
- by taking on another job with more hours instead of their current job(s)
- by accepting an increase in the total number of hours worked in their current job(s) (Simic, 2002)

Time-related underemployment is the form of underemployment typically measured by governments, since it is far easier to quantify than the other forms of underemployment. Using this definition of underemployment, Simic (2002) found that the proportion of the UK workforce who were underemployed between 1997 and 2001 was consistently higher than the proportion of the UK workforce who were unemployed.

Individuals who are in *income-related underemployment* are those who are willing and available to change their current work situation in order to increase their income. Brown and Pintaldi (2006:55) stress the need for "a threshold of adequate income, above which a person cannot be classified as in income-related underemployment" in order to distinguish between those who are truly in need of more income from those who are already well paid but would like to earn more. Instead of using such an absolute threshold, some economists prefer to use a relative standard in which income loss compared to an individual's previous income is a crucial factor (Feldman, 1996).

Individuals who are in *skill-related underemployment* are those who are willing and available to change their current work situation in order to use their current occupational skills more fully. This concept of underemployment as a result of individuals having qualifications and skills in excess of that required by their jobs is essentially the same as the concept of overeducation (Patrinos, 1997; Smith, 1986). Consequently, the terms 'skill-related underemployment' and 'overeducation' will be used interchangeably in this book.

Unlike the previous categories, *status-related underemployment* is not officially recognised by international standards. It is based on the premise that many highly-skilled individuals are concerned about the loss of occupational status they suffer as a result of taking on jobs below their qualification level (Burris, 1983; Friedland & Price, 2003). This aspect of underemployment would appear to be one which may apply to highly-skilled migrants as they negotiate their occupational and social status in a new environment.

The various forms of underemployment are summarised below.

Table 2. Forms of Underemployment

Time-related	mismatch between the number of hours available and the number of hours preferred
Income-related	mismatch between actual earnings and earnings that preclude poverty/earnings to which individual was accustomed
Skill-related	mismatch between individual's acquired education and skill level and that required to carry out the job (= Overeducation)
Status-related	mismatch between the occupational status provided by the job and the occupational status individuals would expect on the basis of their background

Individuals can experience more than one kind of underemployment at the same time. For example, an individual who is working part-time in a position which does not utilise his or her skills fully may be seeking another job which offers more hours and also allows him or her to use his or her skills more fully. This represents an overlap between time-related underemployment and skill-related underemployment (Brown and Pintaldi, 2006).

It is anticipated that these concepts of different types of underemployment will form a useful lens for evaluating the experiences of the highly-skilled migrants in this study. For many, we can surmise that the decision to leave their home country may have been prompted by time-related and income-related underemployment. Whilst their jobs in the destination country may have overcome these inadequacies by providing sufficient hours and a wage perceived as high, they may now experience skill-related underemployment and status-related underemployment, which negatively affect their mental health (Dooley, Prause & Ham-Rowbottom, 2000; Friedland & Price, 2003; Dean & Wilson, 2009) and sense of identity (Trevena, 2006) and may even prompt them to return to their home country.

The decision to move to another country in pursuit of work opportunities has an effect on an individual's career. An examination of such cross-cultural career experience can shed light on a fragmented area of study (Thomas and Inkson, 2007) and add to an understanding of how individuals cope with the challenges and discontinuities of career patterns which are played out in several places and increasingly without organisational support (Arthur & Rousseau, 1996). Our attention therefore now turns to a discussion of career and career transitions.

Career

To define the concept of career is far from straightforward. As Hughes (1997:389) aptly puts it: "Career, the word, has itself had a career." This "term of multi-layered richness and ambiguity" (Collin & Young 2000:1), derived from the Latin *carraria*, meaning a road or carriageway (Arthur and Lawrence,1984:1), implies a sense of direction, and the facilitation of movement to a desired destination (Gowler & Legge, 1989:438). However, there is some disagreement as to the length and nature of this road and the destination to which it leads. In order to understand the concept of career and the ways in which it interrelates with the concepts of mobility and migration which are central to this study, it is necessary for us to establish a definition which addresses the key features of the concept.

One definition which finds much support in the literature is "the evolving sequence of a person's work experience over time" (Arthur, Hall & Lawrence, 1989:8). In contrast with other oft-cited definitions such as "a process of development of the employee along a path of experience and jobs in one or more organizations" (Baruch and Rosenstein, 1992) or "the patterns and sequences of occupations and positions occupied by people across their working lives" (Collin and Young, 2000:3) this definition is broad.

Jepsen and Choudhuri (2001) point out three crucial features of Arthur, Hall & Lawrence's definition. Firstly, its focus on work experiences is broad enough to include productive efforts such as homemaking that do not necessarily involve an employment relationship. Secondly, it places an emphasis on the individual and thirdly, it acknowledges the dimension of time.

These three aspects resonate with Arnold's (1997:16) definition of career as "a sequence of employment related positions, roles, activities and experiences encountered by a person". In this definition, career is seen to include family roles and leisure activities insofar as these link to employment; to be personal with a subjective element; and to unfold over time. A fourth aspect which emerges from Arnold's definition which is of especial interest to the current study is a concern with:

"...how an individual's positions, roles, activities and experiences unfold over time, connect with each other (or not), change in predictable or unpredictable ways, match (or not) a person's changing skills and interests, and enable (or not) a person to expand his or her skills or realize his or her potential." (Arnold, 1997:16 emphasis added)

These four aspects – careers and employment relationships, careers and individuals, careers and time, and careers and discontinuities - provide us with a starting point in our exploration of the concept of career. A further concept which plays an important role in our discussions is that of 'career capital' or the portfolio of resources which aid people in their careers. These resources have been classified into "knowing-why, knowing-how, and knowing-whom" categories which an individual possesses and which affect his or her career. (Arthur et al., 1999).

The question of whether a career should be restricted to employment-related experiences alone has created much debate. Appeals have been made to widen the perspective to embrace both work and non-work role activities and behaviours (Bateson, 1989). Adamson, Doherty & Viney (1998) argue that work career is a subset of life career, arguing that "The concept of career is much broader than the exclusively work-related definitions of career which have dominated management theory and practice for at least the last few decades" (Adamson, Doherty & Viney 1998:253). Indeed, Barley (1989:47) cites several instances in which the Chicago school of sociologists used the term in unusually broad ways "... for instance, the staged logic of a tubercular patient's hospitalisation and recovery (Roth 1963), the plight of a polio victim (Davis 1963), or the process by which inmates of mental hospitals are gradually labeled insane" (Goffman 1961).

New career models (e.g. the boundaryless career, (Arthur & Rousseau, 1996); the protean career, (Hall, 1996) have emerged in response to recent changes in the pattern of work, such as the increased value placed on leisure, increasing unemployment - especially in the manufacturing sector – the rise in the numbers of those employed in part time work, and the increasing feminization of the workplace (The Economist, 30th Dec, 2009). These models acknowledge the role that individuals play outside of organisational boundaries in shaping careers which are "more decoupled from specific organizations, more proactive and enactive ... more portable, more discontinuous, less predictable, and more reliant on improvisation" (Weick, 1996:41). By regarding the individual, not his or her employing organisation, as the owner of his or her career (Kanter 1989), such models place value on flexibility, independence and the willingness to take an idiosyncratic route through one's career. These traits help to account for non-traditional career moves and careers played out outside of organisational boundaries. They reinforce the concept of mobility as central to the development of careers (Forrier, Sels & Stynen, 2009). They have provoked a reconsideration of some conventional careers thinking by questioning the linearity, unidirectionality and upward hierarchy of careers (Lichtenstein and Mendenhall 2002; Brocklehurst, 2003).

Schein (1996), distinguished between 'internally-perceived' (i.e. subjective) versus 'externally prescribed' (i.e. objective) careers. The former involves a subjective sense of where one is going in one's work life, whereas the external career refers to advancement within the organizational hierarchy. Whereas the objective career refers to externally defined reality in the form of visible, observable activities, behaviours, and events in a person's work history, the subjective career is represented by an individual's attitudes, orientations, and perceptions about a career. By the concept of subjective career success is meant an individual's own internal perspective on success, realised through his or her feelings of accomplishment and satisfaction with the progress of his or her career (Judge et al., 1995).

There is increasing evidence that for many expatriates, the internal career appears to take precedence over the external career (Tung, 1998). Nicholson and West (1989) distinguish between the terms "work history" (sequences of job experiences) and "career" (an individual's sense-making story about his or her work history). However, the existence of these two career dimensions does not imply that they exist in isolation. Indeed, Louis (1980) highlights the importance of considering both of these aspects of an individual's career when studying career transitions and research continues into the nature of their interdependence (Arthur, Khapova, & Wilderom, 2005; Khapova et al 2007). Individuals such as those in this study, who may no longer perceive their careers as a progression of jobs within a single profession or institution and who may react in different ways to the challenges they face in their transitions, provide an under-researched context for study (Zikic et al, 2010).

Inherent in the boundaryless and the protean career concepts is a strong emphasis on individual agency and free choice, which is perhaps more relevant to US corporate employees than to intra-Europe migration with its variety of different cultures and languages (Thomas and Inkson, 2007). Within the European context, the boundaryless and the protean career concepts can be said to neglect the importance of structural restrictions resulting from labour market segmentation, institutional rules and regulations, and organizational policies (Forrier, Sels & Stynen, 2009). King, Burke, & Pemberton (2005) highlighted the restrictive role played by employment agencies in limiting the extent to which migrants can use their human capital and other attributes to obtain work.

As Savickas (2002) argues, measuring the differences in a person's career attitudes requires the passage of time and so the notion of development through time is fundamental to the concept of career. This point is supported by Baruch (2004) who points out the meaninglessness of envisaging a career journey without taking into account the concept of time and Sullivan (1999) who argues against the common non-longitudinal approach to the study of careers by stating that "The meaning of one job at one point in time lacks context." (Sullivan 1999:474).

New concepts of career as "boundaryless' (Arthur et al, 1989) and self-driven have raised awareness that careers involve a series of transitions over time, of varying degrees, experienced in a variety of ways (Dany et al., 2003). Those experiencing such transitions may feel "… a sense of renewal and personal growth or, alternatively, a sense of inconsistency and even confusion regarding one's own goals and work values " (Higgins, 2001:595). It is this dynamic characteristic of careers which has awakened interest in examining the discontinuities (Weick, 1995) occurring in individuals' careers. By examining the literature on career transitions, we may be able to illuminate further the relatively under-researched question of how migrants attempt to further or recreate their career in a 'new' home country (Arnold & Cohen, 2008).

Career transitions

This concept of change evolving over time played a central role in Louis' (1980) typology and process model of career transitions in which a career transition was defined as:

"… the period during which an individual is either changing roles (taking on a different objective role) or changing orientation to a role already held (altering a subjective state)" (Louis, 1980:330).

Reviewing the literature, Louis pointed out the need for research into career transitions, from both an objective and a subjective viewpoint.

Louis' (1980) research is widely quoted in expatriate studies (Black, Gregersen & Mendenhall 1992; Harvey 1997; Hippler 2000; Kulkarni, Lengnick-Hall & Valk, 2010; Mendenhall et al, 2008) and its relevance to the ways in which people make sense of novel situations is generally acknowledged. Louis' (1980) transitions framework has been acknowledged in a disparate range of transition studies including retirement of medical technologists and their transitions into other professions (Blau, 2000); organisational commitment among physicians undergoing organisational change (Thompson & van de Ven, 2002); organisational exit (Ebaugh, 1988); and repatriation of Indian expatriates (Kulkarni, Lengnick-Hall & Valk, 2010). Bruce and Scott (1994) tested the validity of Louis' typology across a range of 16 typical transitions, differing in terms of magnitude and desirability, faced by US Naval personnel.

Louis' definition addresses not only the objective aspects of career transitions such as the posts an individual holds and his or her promotions, but also the changes in individuals' subjectively-held views of career, such as shifts in career orientation and altered career expectations. It is this subjective element that is of interest here. An analysis of individuals' subjective views of career is a necessary first step in our attempt to understand what adjustment patterns people can call on in their attempts to cope with the profound changes that career transitions can bring about and how these adjustment patterns affect the individuals involved (Stephens, 1994; Thompson and van de Ven, 2002) .

Louis (1980) identified three constructs at the heart of career transitions: change, contrast, and surprise. Changes are differences in the objective features of the new role and setting, which are "publicly noticeable and knowable, and are often knowable in advance" (Louis 1980:331). Contrasts refer to "perceptual products of the individual's experience in the new setting and role" (Louis 1980:331). Change, then, relates to an external perspective, whereas contrast describes an internal perspective. Unlike the publicly noticeable changes, contrasts are personally noticeable. As such, they are specific to the person and depend on his or her view of a situation. Thus, two people experiencing the same change may experience different contrasts. A further distinction between contrasts and changes is that the former are not usually knowable in advance.

The third construct in Louis' model is that of surprise. This represents the differences between an individual's anticipations of future experiences and the actual events. Surprises provoke both affective and cognitive reactions. Whereas contrasts involve the ability to appreciate subjectively the differences between objective aspects of an old and a new role, surprises involve the ability to appreciate subjectively the differences between one's expectations of a new role and one's subsequent actual experiences. As such, they can be either positive or negative, depending on whether one's expectations are exceeded or fail to be met.

These three key concepts are core to Louis' model of career transitions, since:

> " ... *an appreciation of the varieties of surprise, contrast, and change attendant to career transitions seems essential for understanding and managing transition processes" (Louis, 1980:332).*

Following on from Louis' (1980) work, a model of adjustment to work role transitions was proposed and tested (Nicholson, 1984). Nicholson (1984:173) defined work role transitions as:

> "*any change in employment status and any major change in job content, including all instances of "status passages" ... forms of intra- and interorganizational mobility ... and other changes in employment status (e.g. unemployment, retirement, reemployment)".*

Those transitioning from one career to another expose their identity to challenges. Nicholson (1984) classifies adjustment to role transition as personal development, which leads to changes in one's values and other identity-related attributes. In those cases in which career transitions also involve international relocation, the demands on one's personal development are that much greater. Consequently, we can assume that the act of migration, and the subsequent acculturation process can pose a real threat to the migrants' identities (Timotijevic & Breakwell, 2000; Trevena, 2006). Their sense of identity is challenged by the skill- and status- underemployment in which they find themselves.

Drinkwater, Eade & Garapich (2006) found that Polish graduates in London who were working in low paid jobs interpreted their social standing with respect to different reference points and stratification systems. They often used their UK earnings to increase their Polish capital holdings such as property, and therefore their social standing in Poland. In this way they were able to differentiate between their temporary social position in the UK and their social position in Poland.

Both domestic transitioners contemplating a career move and expatriates deciding whether to accept an overseas assignment expect a lateral or upward transition. However, those who - through choice or desperate necessity - undergo a downward transition face another added layer of complexity as they need to come to terms with the differences between their old and new status, since status affects both social interaction and self-verification (Stryker & Burke, 2000; Sargent, 2003; Timotijevic & Breakwell, 2000).

In order to address the status gap which occurs as a result of migrants' acceptance of jobs which are not commensurate with their qualifications or experience, we have incorporated the related concepts of overeducation and underemployment.

Although much of the transition literature assumes that transitioners would be moving between roles at the same level or from a lower to a higher level, far less attention has been directed at researching the impact of a downward career change on individuals. According to Newman (1999:8):

> *"... when academics study occupational mobility, most of the energy goes into trying to account for upward mobility .... downward mobility [is] ... relegated to footnotes or to a few lines in statistical tables. Rarely is it treated as a topic in its own right."*

Such research as has been conducted into this aspect of transitions reveals several negative aspects on transitioners. Nicholson and West (1988) in their study of male and female managers' career changes, found that individuals who experienced a downward status change showed "major decrements over time in their psychological adjustment and their ratings of work characteristics" (Nicholson & West, 1988:135). Newman (1999) reported that fired executives in the USA admitted to having difficulty in discussing their "descent down the status ladder" (Newman, 1999:11) with their families and friends. Sargent (2003) argued that a downward status change which diminishes job identity would impact both work and career related outcomes, leading to a diminished sense of self, and less effective behaviours within the role.

The lack of focus on downward mobility is perhaps understandable, given the fact that domestic transitions are generally upward or lateral, resulting from individuals' gradually enhanced levels of experience and education. However, whereas citizens of a country may be able to aspire to upward career mobility, this may very well not be the case for those migrating into a foreign country. For such individuals, occupational mobility will vary in accordance with the skills and experience which they bring to their new situation. If these skills do not transfer very well to the new setting, there will be an increased risk of a downward status move. This will be even more likely if migrants suffer any form of discrimination (Rooth & Ekberg, 2006).

Chapter 2: Reasons for migrating

"Why do people move? What makes them uproot and leave everything they've known for a great unknown beyond the horizon? Why climb this Mount Everest of formalities that makes you feel like a beggar? Why enter this jungle of foreignness where everything is new, strange, and difficult? The answer is the same the world over: people move in the hope of a better life." (Yann Martel, (2003) Life of Pi:77)

The concepts of push and pull factors are widely used in studies of motivation to migrate. Pull factors are those aspects of the target country which exert an attraction for potential migrants. In contrast, push factors are those aspects of the home country which drive people away. For example, in a 1998 survey of potential migration in 11 countries in Central and Eastern Europe, Wallace (1999, pp. 27-28) lists five pull factors - living conditions; wages; other people's experiences; good employment; more freedom - and two push factors - ethnic problems and economic conditions - which help to motivate migration. In a review of A8 migrants working in the East of England, McKay & Winkelmann-Gleed (2005) adopt the push/pull factor framework, listing pull factors such as stable UK work prospects and large numbers of compatriots with good experiences working in the UK and push factors such as high home country unemployment and low wages in the home country as instrumental in migrant workers' decision to seek work in the UK. Dickinson et al (2008) contrast the 'pull' of economic strengths and widespread vacancies in the UK with the 'push' of struggling home country economies and widespread home country unemployment. Such push and pull factors will, then, play a role in an individual's decision to seek work overseas.

The basic concept of push and pull forces finds a great deal of support within other theories. For example, Neoclassical Economics Theory emphasises the influence of economic pull factors on the decision to migrate by rational actors seeking to improve their wellbeing by relocating to countries or regions in which their labour will be rewarded at a higher level than in their home country or region (Todaro, 1980). The principle of accepting costs in order to make higher future returns conceptualises migration as a form of investment of human capital (Arango, 2000).

Neoclassical Economics Theory postulates that individuals strive to migrate to places in which their anticipated net returns are greatest (Borjas, 1994; Massey et al., 1993; Massey, 1998).

Disputing the emphasis that Neoclassical Economics Theory places on economic pull factors, Arango (2000:286) argues that due to recent changes in the nature of migration patterns, political factors are "much more influential than differential wages in determining mobility or immobility." Nevertheless, there are also criticisms pointing out the simplicity of push/pull models which fail to reflect the dynamic nature of the "process" which is largely based on insecurities –i.e. reflections of conflicts at the places of origin (Sirkeci, 2009; Cohen and Sirkeci, 2011).

The potential economic advantages of a job in the UK clearly exert "a strong pull factor in many initial decisions to migrate" (Cook, Dwyer & Waite, 2011: 60). However, economic reasons alone do not fully account for a migrant's decision to come to the UK. The neo-classical claim that migration is brought about by a rational decision to enhance income is questioned by Arango (2000) who argues that, were migration flows to conform with the tenets of neo-classical migration theory, there would be a substantially greater number of migrants than the 191 million people or 3 per cent of the world's population who lived outside their country of origin in 2005 (UNFPA, 2005).

Cook, Dwyer & Waite (2011:55) question the widespread depiction of A8 migrants as "short-term economic opportunists" arguing that "the factors underpinning the migration of many A8 migrants are more complicated." Migrants may also be attracted by non-economic pull factors such as "better working conditions, increased career opportunities, travel opportunities and greater personal freedom" (Bell, Jarman & Lefebvre, 2004: 48). Green, Owen and Jones (2008) cite interviewees who put equal weight on economic and non-economic factors (e.g. social networking, the opportunity to learn English). For some migrants, the appeal of coming to the UK is less definable, expressed merely as an 'adventure' (Schneider & Holman, 2009; McKay & Winkelmann-Gleed, 2005; Trevena, 2009).

Kazlauskiene & Rinkevicius (2006) argue that the desire for professional recognition may also be a strong pull factor. This is also true for less permanent mobility patterns; Balter (1999) points out that European PhD holders who wish to become academic researchers place great value on periods abroad. Bell, Jarman & Lefebvre (2004) found that nurses chose to work in Northern Ireland partly because it offered them the opportunity of working in well-established hospitals in which they could enhance their skills, and so improve their long-term career prospects.

A more recent enhancement of neoclassical economics, the New

Economics of Labour Migration theory (NELM), identifies the family or household as exerting a push factor in the migration process. Migration is seen as a family-led strategy which aims not merely to maximise individual income, but to minimise risks such as unemployment and to evade market failures (Howe et al, 2004). By diversifying the work location of its members, households are able to decrease the economic risks they face. Because not all the members of the family work in the local market, should the local economy become depressed and unable to supply enough income, the whole family can depend on remittances provided by those members working in the foreign labour markets (Taylor, 1999). When an individual reaches a decision to migrate this may not be a purely personal decision or even one in the best interests of the individual. Rather, it may reflect the desire of a larger family unit to improve its well-being by receiving remittances from relatives working abroad (Bauer, Haisken-DeNew & Schmidt, 2004).

In their survey of 416 Lithuanians working overseas, Kazlauskiene and Rinkevcius (2006) found that unsatisfactory wages and scarce possibilities for professional realisation played an important role in the decision to migrate. They further pointed out that this was most prevalent among those who had been unable to find employment and those who were only in temporary employment. The proposition that the unemployed have a higher propensity to migrate than the employed is well supported (Goss & Schoening, 1984; Hughes & McCormick, 1985; Fischer & Malmberg, 2001).

The idea that dissatisfaction with one's place of residence has an impact in the decision to move is supported by the "place utility" framework of migration decision making (Wolpert, 1965; Heaton, Clifford & Fuguitt, 1981; Speare, Kobrin, & Kingkade, 1982; De Jong, Chamratrithirong, & Tran, 2002; Sirkeci, 2009).

However, the effect that many of the forces have on an individual's decision to migrate is dependent in part upon personal factors. Some of these are general, such as how open individuals are to change or what prior experience they have of migration (Cohen and Sirkeci, 2011). Others may be the result of people's age, education, gender, or race. It is important to recognise that it is the perception which individuals have of factors - not the actual factors themselves - which determines their decisions. This allows us to explain why, in a given situation at the origin, "… individual A migrates, while otherwise comparable B does not" (Greenwood, 1997:694).

The intervening obstacles provide varying levels of resistance to be overcome too. For example, obstacles such as distance and concomitant relocation costs can be overcome relatively easily in comparison to restrictive immigration laws or racial quotas. The intervening obstacles may also impact in varying degrees on different people; some may more easily overcome the obstacle of travelling costs than others without the resources to do so, for example.

A factor which is frequently mentioned in the international migration literature (Massey & Sanchez, 2010) is the existence of a network of relatives and friends who have previously migrated to the receiving country. In itself, the existence of such a network is not considered enough to trigger the decision to migrate (Boneva & Frieze, 2001). However, the ties that exist between potential migrants and their family and friends already in situ form a resource which facilitates their migration to and settlement in the receiving country, once the decision to migrate has been taken.

Relatives and friends already in the destination country help new migrants to find jobs and provide social and cultural support within a familiar migrant community (Faist, 1997). In a cross-national survey examining the willingness to move of residents from several Central and Eastern European Countries, Drinkwater (2003) reports that the willingness to move of individuals who have spent any time living abroad is significantly higher than those who have not previously lived outside of their home country. Ackers (2004) pointed out that scientists moving overseas at an early age with their family, and those whose school or undergraduate studies included time spent abroad, are more inclined to move again in the future. Palloni et al (2001) found that the likelihood of migration of Mexicans to the United States tripled if they had an older sibling who had already migrated there. The existence of a network of family and/or friends in situ allows potential migrants to form a realistic picture before deciding to migrate.

Networks of migrants in the destination country create migration momentum, thus perpetuating migration despite falling standards in the destination country or improving standards at home, which, according to the neoclassical view, would obviate against it (Boyd, 1989; Howe et al., 2004). The momentum provided by migrant networks helps to explain why governments find it easier to prevent immigration before it begins than to close it down once it has begun (Howe et al., 2004).

Cumulative Causation theory (Massey, 1990; Myrdal, 1957) holds that migration changes values and cultural perceptions in ways that increase the probability of future migration. The perception of the act of migration may shift in the community in the country of origin, with the strictly economic nature of the act yielding to the idea of "a rite of passage for young men." (Herman, 2006:197). Additionally, an increasing number of migrants sending remittances back to their home country will increase the living standards of their families. This will accelerate migration since other members of the community in the home country experience further relative deprivation, increasing the likelihood that they will also migrate (Howe et al., 2004).

The decision to migrate, then, is a complex one (McKay & Winkelmann-Gleed, 2005; Robinson & Carey, 2000), which combines push and pull factors viewed from a personal, family, social and economic level (Ferro, 2006). Equally complex, but less frequently studied, are the reasons why migration does *not* occur (Faist 2000; Ferro, 2006; Hammar & Tamas 1997; Tassinopoulos & Werner, 1999) and so we must now examine factors which may dissuade potential migrants from relocating.

Migration is not an easy option. Those who are considering migrating without prior experience form a picture in their mind as to the benefits of migrating which may, in the absence of first-hand experience, be inaccurate and misleading. For example, Benson-Rea and Rawlinson (2003) claim that the lack of accurate and realistic information about employment and business conditions available to prospective migrants to New Zealand leads to dissatisfaction. They cite Oliver's (2000) finding that migrants in New Zealand had been under the false impression that they would obtain employment commensurate in status and pay to the status they had enjoyed in their home country.

There are several obstacles for the prospective migrant such as distance, physical and political barriers, and family status. Lee (1966) highlights the selective nature of the migration process in which individuals' responses to push-pull factors are influenced by differentials such as social class, age, and gender. These differentials determine their ability to overcome intervening obstacles.

Political barriers, such as national immigration restrictions, which have an inhibitive effect on potential migratory movements, should not be evident between EU member states. However, although the lack of restrictions on free movement serves to encourage mobility within the EU, the EU nation states have generally discouraged non-EU citizens from entering the EU. This creates an intervening obstacle for non-EU migrants but not for EU migrants.

Despite the lack of entry barriers, other institutional barriers exist. Professional associations and hiring bodies, for example, may find fault with immigrants' credentials and create barriers preventing them from entering their chosen profession (Bauder, 2003). Pemberton (2008) found that employment agencies in the North West of England pushed migrants into accepting initial 'foot in the door' unskilled work offers which did not take account of their skills. Even in the event that the qualifications are deemed acceptable, other factors may come into play. Employers may rule out qualified applicants based on lack of relevant (i.e. local) work experience (Friedberg, 2000; Kler, 2006); perceived ability to fit in or to project an appropriate corporate image to customers (Watson, 1996); or lack of adequate 'soft skills' such as zeal for constant learning, the ability to think ahead, teamwork and flexibility (Shih, 2002; Schneider & Holman, 2005).

Faced with such barriers to employment, migrants may opt to set themselves up in business, resulting in relatively high rates of entrepreneurship among migrant groups (Clark & Drinkwater, 2010). In the years leading up to accession, migrants from Eastern Europe could enter the UK if they had self employed status. Once this was no longer a prerequisite after accession, the self employed ratio of the workforce plummeted (Drinkwater, Eade & Garapich, 2006).

Age can play a role. The 'psychic costs' of learning a new language and culture, adapting to a new labour market, losing touch with old contacts and making new ones (Massey et al., 1993) of older migrants may be higher since they generally find it much more difficult to adapt, especially in terms of learning the language (Battu and Sloane, 2002; Dustmann and Fabbri, 2003).

A further obstacle which might dissuade potential migrants from committing to a move is the existence of strong family ties in the country of origin. The decision for a family member (usually male) to relocate and leave family behind can be traumatic. A recent study of Polish migrants working in Scotland (Weishaar, 2008) found that separation from extended family in the home country was a source of anxiety.

The usefulness of economic and environmental factors in accounting for the desire to emigrate is questioned by Boneva and Frieze (2001) who stress the importance of personal factors, arguing that a certain pattern of personality characteristics is predictive of a greater desire to emigrate. They propose that this desire could be triggered by a high level of achievement motivation and/or power motivation whereas the desire to remain in the home country could be due to a high level of affiliation motivation. The personality pattern of the potential migrant interacts with environmental factors and opportunities in such a way that only those whose personality pattern means that they have the desire to migrate actually do so.

The value in establishing such traits in migrants would lie in helping them to carry out tasks and activities in the target country to fulfil their heightened psychological needs. For example, those with high power orientation could be given roles within community groups (Boneva and Frieze, 2001). As Gans (1999), however, points out, the evidence for a migrant personality is not great. Furthermore, as proponents of NELM point out, the decision to migrate in search of work is not taken in a vacuum but is often made on a family level, in which individual personality traits may not play a role or may be overridden in the interest of the family as a whole.

The non-permanent nature of the international movement of EU citizens, with their freedom of movement allowing them to return at will to their home country, could arguably negate the need for a certain set of personality traits to be required in order to undertake an international relocation. Since a visit to another country would be non-binding, it could be argued that those with lower achievement motivation may be more willing to seek work elsewhere and those with high affiliation motivation might be comforted by the ease with which they could return to their family environment, should they feel the need to do so.

Carling's (2002) concept of "involuntary immobility", represents friction between the *desire* to migrate and the *inability* to do so. This is an important concept when contrasted with the neoclassical migration theory, which implies that any non-migration is arrived at by a logical assessment of a lack of the potential benefits of migrating. However, as Carling explains, a series of macro and micro level factors can come into play to thwart migrants' aspiration to migrate.

Macro level factors include the socially constructed meaning of migration and the emigration environment, consisting of the historical, social, economic, cultural or political setting which encourages or discourages migration. Micro level factors, such as gender, age, family migration history, social status, educational attainment and personality traits, influence individuals' migration aspirations. Carling's model represents an empirical tool for the study of the pre-migration stage, and allows for the conditions and determining factors that affect people's choices and opportunities to move to be taken into consideration (Ferro, 2006).

Carling's model helps to shed light on the distinction between EU and non-EU migrants. Political barriers created to restrict non-EU immigration can thwart the ambitions of individuals to seek work in the UK. For EU citizens, such as those in this study, this barrier does not exist. While the absence of such barriers can promote migration, their existence can also prevent or restrict it.

Intra-EU migration

An appreciation of the forces driving and sustaining migration is important in helping us to understand the decision of the migrants in this study to seek work in the UK. However, since the Treaty of Rome was signed in 1957, the right of freedom of movement throughout the EU for EU citizens and their families has been one of the core 'acquis' of the European Communities (Currie, 2006). Within the EU, this has helped to bring about changing patterns of mobility in which 'one-off' movements leading to permanent resettlement have given way to more fluid practices of international mobility involving alternating residence in different countries (Pennix et al, 2008).

In 2006, designated the European Year of Workers' Mobility, Vladimír

Špidla, the EU Commissioner for Employment, Social Affairs and Equal Opportunities, put forth an impassioned call for a more mobile workforce, equipped to learn new skills and adapt to new environments in order to meet the EU's growth and jobs strategy (Vandenbrande et al, 2006). The European Foundation for the Improvement of Living and Working Conditions (2006:1) stressed the importance of greater mobility within the EU in order to increase the community's competitive ability in the face of "the growing challenges of globalisation, rapid technological change and a developing knowledge society". Such objectives imply an efficient and constructive community-wide utilisation of human capital.

Such lofty ideals may not be realised by all those who relocate within the EU. In a study of highly-skilled Eastern Europeans in Denmark, Liversage (2009: 204) pointed out the difficulty in understanding:

> *"the complex unfolding processes of entering new labour markets through which some gain access to resources while others fail - how some immigrants find good jobs while others become the proverbial highly educated taxi drivers."*

Felker (2011) identified the degree to which potential movers research the job market and career opportunities in the UK before moving as one possible way in which they might find such good jobs. The migrant workers in her study, although highly qualified, did not appear to put much thought into their move to the UK. Rather than research the job market and professional opportunities, they seemed to be content to adopt a wait and see approach. Lack of preparation and pre-departure planning could, then, negatively impact on migrants' ability to find jobs which are commensurate with their abilities and qualifications.

Another reason for failure to find good jobs is an inability to learn the requisite skills. Although many A8 migrants have indeed been learning new skills, these have very often been at a far lower level than their qualifications and experience would suggest. As Felker (2011) points out, the learning experiences of individuals who find themselves in skill- and status- related underemployment, if indeed they are useful at all, are more likely to add to their cultural awareness rather than to provide them with knowledge and skills which are of direct relevance to their careers.

Schneider & Holman (2005) found that in Norfolk, most migrant workers, particularly females, were unable to use employment skills matching identified shortages in the construction sector and had, instead, to accept jobs at a lower skill level. This mismatch between the desire for a mobile, highly-skilled European workforce and the reality of highly-skilled migrants in a situation of 'brain waste' questions the benefits, both to workers and to member countries, of the EU's growth strategy.

As Currie (2007) argues, since the 2004 EU enlargement, A8 migrants have begun to take on work roles more similar to those traditionally filled by third-country nationals, namely 'degrading, dangerous and dirty' work shunned by the citizens of the EU-15 nations. According to a 2009 Home Office report, the occupations most frequently entered by A8 migrant workers in the UK between July 2004 and March 2009 were:
Process operative (other factory worker)
Warehouse Operative
Packer
Kitchen and catering assistants
Cleaner, domestic staff
Farm worker/ Farm hand
Waiter/waitress
Maid / Room attendant (hotel)
Sales and retail assistants
Labourer, building
(Home Office, 2009)

Despite the high frequency of such manual occupations taken on by the migrants, in many cases such jobs did not correspond to their abilities and qualifications (Schneider & Holman, 2005; Bell, Jarman, & Lefebvre, 2004; bSolutions, 2005; Zaronaite and Tirzite 2005).
The lack of recognition in destination countries of qualifications obtained in migrants' home countries adversely affects migrants in the UK. As Shah and Long (2009) make clear, the increasing bonds between the countries of the European Union do little to alleviate this problem since little progress has been made towards an EU-wide system of mutual recognition of qualifications and skills. Zaronaite and Tirzite (2005:12) bemoan the fact that "many highly qualified migrant workers, such as engineers, teachers, doctors are working in pack houses." They attribute this to lack of recognition of migrants' qualifications, a theme echoed in other studies (Currie, 2007; Pemberton, 2008). The European Commission (2013) stress the need for the qualifications of mobile EU professionals to be recognised in a fast, simple and reliable way.
According to Currie (2007), although the EU has developed a system of mutual recognition of qualifications and non-discrimination, this emphasises recognition of professional qualifications over general educational or academic qualifications. Consequently, migrants from within the EU may find their qualifications devalued in another member state. This view is reinforced by a Europe-wide study (Barone, 2009) which stresses the widespread existence in several European countries of problems in

recognising migrant workers' educational credentials and points out that the lack of reference in UK legislation to migrant workers' qualifications and skills adversely affects their full integration into the workplace (Barone, 2009).

Highly-skilled migrants have to come to terms with an unfamiliar social, cultural and economic environment. The barriers that they face include lack of recognition of qualifications, lack of local skills and language, and a lack of familiarity with local structures and institutional procedures (Zikic, Bonache and Cerdin, 2010; Syed, 2008).

This study, however, does not address the nature of such obstacles which confront the migrants. Rather, the central interest in this study is the nature of the response of the migrants to these obstacles.

Chapter 3: The Migrants

The following pages provide an overview of the participants in this study. There was a wide range of ages, nationalities and backgrounds within the sample. Interviewees also differed in the length of time they had spent in the UK prior to interview, and the number of times they had visited the UK. In the vast majority of cases, the jobs they were doing at the time of the interview were clearly not commensurate with their background and qualifications.

Table 3. Interviewee profiles

Marital Status	Single	7	Gender	Female	11
	Married	12		Male	8
Age groups	25-30	9	Time in the UK	< 2 years	8
	31-35	5		2-3 years	4
	36-40	1		3-4 years	2
	41-50	1		4-5 years	2
	51-55	2		5 years +	3
	55+	1			
Nationalities	Brazilian/ Portuguese	1	Latvian	2	
	Iranian/Dutch	1	Brazilian/ Italian	2	
	French	1			
	Lithuanian	2	Polish	9	
	Portuguese	1			

Andrzej

Andrzej was single, from Poland, and in his mid-30s. At the time of the interview, he had been in the UK for 21 months and was leaving for good that very night. He had graduated from a prestigious faculty of veterinary medicine in Poland and practised there as a vet for some five years. His decision to come to the UK was based on urgent financial need after he had been unable to repay a debt he had taken out in Poland in order to support his veterinary clinic.

He arrived without a job and survived in London on only £300 capital, advertising his veterinary services to fellow Poles, and looking for work on the Internet, which he accessed by visiting Internet cafes. He was able to procure a job in the East Midlands which he saw advertised on the Internet. The job involved working with animals in a laboratory. Andrzej was fired from this job on a technicality but bore a grudge because he believed he was dismissed because he was more knowledgeable about animal care than his supervisors. He tried hard to procure jobs in veterinary clinics in the area but to no avail.

He subsequently took on jobs in a factory and as a security guard, at one stage working up to 80 hours a week. On arrival, Andrzej had next to no English and although he attended some classes as far as his busy schedule would allow, he was frustrated that his English was not progressing very well. He attributed this lack of progress to living and socialising solely with Polish people.

Andrzej had originally planned to stay two years but had managed to pay off most of his debt and was growing increasingly frustrated at not being able to work with animals. He had been able to obtain a job in Poland as a prophylactic veterinarian on a farm.

Despite his unhappiness in the UK, Andrzej and his fiancée in Poland were considering returning to the UK once they had started a family, so that their children and Andrzej could improve their command of the English language.

Brigita

Brigita was in her mid-50s, came from Lithuania, and was married with three children aged 23, 20 and 15. She had graduated in medicine and had worked in a first aid medical station in Lithuania for 25 years. She had been persuaded by a fellow doctor who had left Lithuania for the UK that she would be able to practice medicine in the UK. However, the agency she applied through in Lithuania placed her in a care home in the West Midlands as an assistant, a job which she had remained in for the 18 months since her arrival.

Shortly after her arrival, her husband, and her 15-year-old daughter and 20-year-old son joined her. At the time of the interview, their daughter was in the process of being considered for acceptance into Birmingham Conservatoire and the son was applying for a UK university place. Brigita herself was also studying at university on a pre-adaptation program for health professionals, on conclusion of which she hoped to find a position in the NHS. At the time of the interview, she was attempting to find voluntary work in addition to her study and her job in order to bolster her CV.

Brigita's husband, a computer engineer, was working in a warehouse whilst looking for more suitable employment. He was also learning English as he had only a basic knowledge of the language. Brigita felt very highly motivated to stay in the UK for the sake of their children's education. She was very hopeful of finding more suitable employment and planned to stay in the UK for at least another five years.

Cecylja

Cecylja was in her early 30s, single, and from Poland. At the time of the interview, she had been living in the UK for about two and a half years. Since completing her university study in pedagogy in Poland, she had been doing temporary administrative work in offices there. She decided that she would look for work in the UK, primarily in order to earn more money, but also because she wanted to improve her English. She was able to find work through an agency in Poland, who placed her in a warehouse in the East Midlands. She found this job demanding due to an injury to her back which she had incurred as a swimming coach in her home country.

Eighteen months before the interview, Cecylja had been offered a permanent job in a works canteen, and had left her temporary administrative post in a marketing agency as she longed for the security of a permanent job. A further advantage for her was that the hours of work were fixed and with a regular income she was able to afford the time and cost to take English lessons. At the time of the interview she was growing in confidence in her ability to converse in English and was contemplating looking for other work.

Cecylja was contemplating returning to Poland in the next two or three years, and she was confident that the job market and the general political climate there would improve. Although she was happy in her canteen work, she felt that she could not remain in this job for too long if she were to be eligible for any more suitable jobs in the future.

Celine

Celine was in her mid-30s, in a permanent relationship with a UK national, and from France. She had first come to the UK fifteen years previously after finishing her Master's degree in Geography and Cartography. She was unemployed at the time and eager for an adventure after her studies and accepted a job as an au-pair in Surrey. Eighteen months later she found a job in the East Midlands as a cartographer until she was made redundant six years later.

After several years of being unable to find work, except for part-time translation work and being unwilling to move away from her partner to seek work, she enrolled on a PGCE course. She passed the course but failed her teaching placements. At the time of the interview, she was working as a teaching assistant in a school in the East Midlands, where she felt unsatisfied

41

with her status. However, she enjoyed the work she was doing and did not feel it placed too many demands on her.

Celine has no close ties to any remaining family in France and feels more British than French. She intends to stay in the UK permanently, although she is not sure how long she will remain in her current post or whether she will be able to find alternative employment.

Edmund

Edmund is in his late 20s, Polish, and married to Marjanna (see below). After finishing his studies in Poland, he qualified professionally in computer networking and worked in the computer industry both on an employed and self-employed basis. At the time of the interview, he had been living in the UK for two years. His wife joined him after six months.

His decision to come to the UK was not one to which he had given any great consideration. His sister was living here and invited him over, urging him to see how he felt about working over here. After several temporary jobs, he was able to procure a post with the police through an agency. He then applied internally for a more responsible position following the retirement of the previous post holder and took on some of these duties in addition to his own before officially taking the job.

Since being in this post, he has been called upon to put some of his computer skills to use and is filling in for an absent colleague as well as doing his job. He lives close to a number of relatives and in-laws and tends to shun the company of workmates or English acquaintances.

He is happy in his work but still trying to find even more suitable employment. He and his wife have a vague plan to set up a Polish restaurant or food store. Edmund has the intention of remaining in the UK for another few years or until things improve politically and economically in Poland.

Gabriela

Gabriela is originally from Brazil but also holds a Portuguese passport as her parents were born in Portugal. She is in her early 30s, in her second marriage, and lives in the East Midlands with her parents and three children aged 10 years, four years and nine months. Her husband was currently experiencing difficulties in obtaining a visa.

Gabriela converted to Islam a few years before coming to the UK and experienced religious harassment in Brazil. She decided to visit a part of the UK which she knew to be predominantly populated by Muslims. She decided to visit and while there, she was offered employment. She decided to stay in order to be able to practice her religion freely and because she thought it was better for her children.

Gabriella had qualified and worked as a vet in Brazil, but after completing an internship in the United Nations in Rio de Janeiro, she felt she wanted a career change. Also in Brazil, she had attended night class in order to complete a BA in International Relations. Her ambition was to enrol on a postgraduate course in International Relations in the local university.

At the time of the interview, she had been in the UK for eighteen months and was busily studying for the IELTS examination in order to be accepted on the postgraduate course. She had no fixed plans after this year of study would be completed. However with her parents and children settled, she did not anticipate returning to Brazil or Portugal.

Isabella

Isabella was in her late 30s, single and from Portugal. At the time of the interview, she had been in the UK for five years. Before coming to the UK, she had been studying, although she had spent a lot of time travelling, including an extended period in Belgium, where her father lived, during which time she worked in sales.

Her motive in coming to the UK was to earn enough money to continue her studies by distance from Portugal. Before coming to the UK, she had accepted a job she had seen advertised in a Road Chef, but was currently working as a caretaker in a school in the East Midlands.

She was having difficulties in combining work and study and at the time of the interview was not really clear as to how long she would remain in the UK or in her present job. However her aspiration was to earn enough money to be able to dedicate herself to her studies and finish her degree once and for all.

Jiri

Jiri was in his late 50s, married with two children aged 20 and 18. He held Polish nationality, but lived in the Czech Republic. His wife did not accompany him to the UK, and although she visited him on a couple of occasions, she was not too happy at his decision to work and live here.

Jiri was a pathologist, although he had not completed all of the necessary degrees. In 2005, he was made redundant, and found it impossible to find alternative work of a similar nature in the Czech Republic. He decided to come to the UK after his daughter had spent two months working in the East Midlands and had given him a favourable report.

At the time of the interview, Jiri had been working in the UK for two years and was employed in a warehouse, where he was required to sort goods. Especially at first, he found the work very demanding physically. He lived in fear of losing his job because of the very strict on-the-job efficiency requirements placed upon him and his fear that he would be unable to find other work here, partly because of his age.

He was very happy with the financial package he was on, and had every intention of staying in the job as long as he could, with no immediate plans to return to the Czech Republic.

Juliana

Juliana was Brazilian but held an Italian passport. Before coming to the UK, she travelled with her husband Ricardo (see below), to Germany, where they had been working in an ice cream shop, regularly putting in 16-hour days. They found it very demanding, and had heard from Brazilian friends in the UK that work was easier here. They then travelled to the East of England where they had been working for one and a half years at the time of the interview.

Juliana was not very confident in her use of English, but felt that she was making progress here. She and husband were working in a pizza packing factory. She felt that they were treated like animals in this job, and found it physically very demanding, having to work standing up for long periods in temperatures as low as 4°C.

Juliana had been a journalist and reporter in Brazil. Together with her husband, her reason for leaving her home country was financial, since they wanted to pay off a mortgage on a newly built flat within three years. At the time of the interview their financial plan was on track, and they were certain that they would leave just as soon as the last payment was made.

Kamal

Kamal is originally from Iran but was granted political asylum in Holland, where he had to spend three years in a refugee camp. A clinical psychologist by training, he retrained following his successful asylum and took a job as a network administrator for Médecins Sans Frontières in Den Haag. In his early 40s, and married with a six-year-old daughter, at the time of interview he had been in the UK for 4 years.

Despite his success in finding rewarding employment in Holland, he became frustrated with life there. His wife was increasingly keen to live in the UK, where she had several family members. Eventually, not completely wholeheartedly, Kamal set off alone to England to seek work.

He eventually found work in a chicken factory as a quality controller, but was horrified by his experiences there. Whilst there, he became increasingly involved in union activity and was delighted when he passed an interview to become a union organiser for a large trade union based in the West Midlands.

He has since been joined by his wife and his daughter, and, although he enjoys his job, he is somewhat concerned at the standard of his daughter's school. He is currently studying, under the sponsorship of the union, to pass the IELTS exam in order to enrol on postgraduate study. He is resigned to remaining in the UK, where his wife is very happy.

Marjanna

Marjanna is married to Edmund, (see above) whom she followed to the UK after he had been here for about six months. At this time she was finishing her final degree examinations in accountancy in Warsaw. In her late 20s, she arrived in the UK freshly married and about to graduate but unable to find suitable work.

Having worked during her studies as a waitress, she found work in a coffee shop, where she had been for over a year at the time of the interview. Although she was happy in this work, she was frustrated at her inability to find work related to her studies, and was considering resigning from the job in order to try to find more suitable work.

She had several family members nearby and was quite happy to remain in the UK in the short to medium term, although she was becoming increasingly frustrated at the nature of her work.

Ona

Ona was in her late 20s, from Lithuania, married with a four-year old child. In her home country she had been working as a fully qualified lab assistant, but, after being made redundant, she was having difficulty in finding suitable work. Being unable to work in her chosen profession, she took on a job in a hardware store in Lithuania and then decided that there was nothing to lose by looking for work in the UK. She obtained a job working in the onion fields in Lincolnshire through an agency.

She was so horrified by the conditions there that she walked out after one day and found work in a chicken factory. Despite being able to obtain a job as a quality controller there, she found it difficult to work with the predominantly Asian workforce and became heavily involved with the union after filing sexual harassment charges.

At the time of the interview, some four years after her arrival, she was working for a trade union in the West Midlands. Her family was with her in the UK. She was a little disappointed in her child's education but reasonably happy to remain in the UK in the medium to long term. She believed that the job she was doing was in a worthwhile cause.

Pawel

Pawel was in his late 20s, single on arrival, having since entered into a civil partnership in the UK. Before coming to the UK, Pawel was an English teacher in Poland, where he graduated with a BA in English. As well as teaching, he had been working part-time as a recruitment consultant.

He described his motivation in going to England as mainly 'a bit of an adventure'. He had visited before, was fluent in the language, and had a long two-month vacation from school. At the end of this period, he decided he wanted to stay in the UK, and although he was promised work teaching, this failed to materialise as he was unable to provide the necessary paperwork requested by the agency.

Apart from some part time and poorly paid translating work, and some time spent working as a gardener, he decided to offer his services as a freelance painter and decorator. A short six months later, he had started his own painting and decorating business, and was employing six people.

He had already begun plans for a second business, helping people relocate to and from Poland. He felt it would be very difficult to live with a same sex partner in Poland. The couple were contemplating moving to an Asian country such as Thailand, in order to see whether they preferred the lifestyle there.

Ricardo

Ricardo is Brazilian, but has an Italian passport. He was in his early 30s, and came to the UK with his wife Juliana (see above). In Brazil he was qualified as a system analyst but had been working as an administrator in an advertising agency there. He and his wife left Brazil for Germany to work in an ice cream shop. However, the demands of the work were too heavy, and they decided to come to England instead.

They had a fixed financial plan in order to repay a mortgage, and were planning to leave after the last payment was made.

Sebastian

Sebastian was in his mid-20s, single, and had completed a Masters degree in music in Poland. He had been working on a freelance basis in his home country authoring music scores for theatres, films and advertisements, as well as working in a recording studio as a sound engineer.

His reason for coming to the UK was to raise money for studies in musicology in Amsterdam, where his girlfriend was studying. He was also invited over here by his friend Stanislaw (see below). At the time of the interview, he had been in the UK for three months. He was working in a factory and intended to leave in another six months.

Sofija

Sofija was in her late 20s, single, and had arrived from Latvia some three years previously. Having graduated from administrative college, she had been working for the Army in her home country. However, following reorganisation she was made redundant, and then spent a year looking for other work. In this time, she re-qualified as a technical lab analyst but became disillusioned with the short-term nature of the work she was able to find in Latvia.

She came over to the East of England with her then boyfriend to stay with his aunt and look for work. Despite not having very much English when she arrived, Sofija worked extremely hard to improve her command of the language, and was offered a promotion to an administrative position in the factory where she worked.

Whilst here, she became engaged to a South African, and they were contemplating moving to South Africa in the near future.

Stanislaw

Stanislaw was in his early 30s, single, with dual Polish and German nationality. He had studied Economics at University before transferring to the Social Science department, having developed a strong interest in Anthropology. Before coming to the UK, he had travelled to other countries in Europe to work, but then returned to help in the family business in Poland. Some two years before the interview, he had felt that he had no choice but to seek work in the UK when his mother fell ill with cancer and they needed to raise money urgently for an operation.

Stanislaw worked in the same laboratory as Andrzej, (see above), from which he was also fired. Since that time he had been doing a number of jobs in factories, and was becoming somewhat disillusioned with his co-workers. He had worked very hard at improving his English from a fairly low-level to a level at which he felt he would be able to hold down a more meaningful job. At the time of the interview, he was applying for such jobs and felt confident that he would be able to find one.

Nevertheless, now that his immediate financial crisis had been averted, he was seriously considering returning to Poland, where he had been offered some interesting jobs in cultural centres.

Valeska

Valeska was in her early 50s, and arrived in the UK without her husband, who remained in Poland. Since graduating several years previously in Pedagogy and Re-socialisation, she had had various jobs, mainly in the healthcare industry. However, for the last five years, she had had great difficulty in finding work, and felt that this was a social stigma in Poland.

She accepted a job from an agency in Poland, working in a care home in the East Midlands, but was dismissed from this job following an accusation of mistreating a patient. She then took on a series of factory jobs, but found it increasingly difficult to settle in any of these. She became very disillusioned with the whole notion of work.

Her great interest was learning English, and she was frustrated that she was unable to attend classes very often because of the arbitrary nature of her temporary work schedule. She was hoping to save a little more money before returning to Poland in another six months or so.

Veronika

Veronika was in her 20s, single, and had arrived from Latvia five and a half years previously. Before that she had been working in the UK as a student, picking strawberries on a farm. After a few months she returned to Latvia to finish her studies. After graduating, she was unable to find suitable employment in Latvia, and decided to return to the UK. Once again, she was working on a farm picking strawberries.

After some time she got a job in a packhouse, then a print room. During this time, she attended college, and gradually gained confidence in her command of English and subject knowledge within her specialised area of Economics and Law. When she saw a job advertised with the local council, to carry out a survey of migrant workers in the area and make recommendations, she decided to apply. Having been accepted, she was able to successfully apply for a second two-year project with the council, implementing the recommendations from her survey.

At the time of the interview, this second two-year period was coming to an end, and Veronika was unsure of the future. Having brought her family (parents and brother) over and having bought a house in the East of England, she was committed to staying in the UK, but unsure as to what kind of work she would be able to procure.

Chapter 4: Factors influencing the migrant workers' decision to come to the UK to take up or seek work

Pull factors

A common theme in migrant workers' stories is the sense of adventure, in which the decision to come to the UK is seen as a chance to experience "something new" - a "challenge" which would perhaps lead in unexpected directions. This was mentioned by four of the interviewees in this study.

Celine came to the UK fifteen years ago, after completing her Master's in France at the age of 23. At the time, she had not given much thought to what she would do:

"I think when I came here I was very open minded. I had this vague plan, I'd go to England for a year then I'd be to Germany for six months and then maybe to Italy for six months and after that maybe I get this wonderful job working for the United Nations or something [laughs] and that didn't happen."

This sense of spontaneity leading to a decision to travel, following the ending of an extended event in the interviewee's life, was echoed by Pawel. Whereas Celine had just finished her Master's degree, Pawel had just finished teaching at the end of the school year and on a whim:

I, actually I came.. with no reason of staying, I just came 'cos at that time in Poland I used to work as a teacher in secondary school and because we had like two months holiday, I decided to have like one more holiday adventure and just see how, how it would be ..... More like a holiday adventure.

Sofija had been made redundant and failed in her attempts to find any full time employment in Latvia. Her decision was one which she felt did not impact on any significant others and so one she was willing to try:

I had the opportunity to come over and I thought that, because I don't have any family like children and husband, so I'm like single, I can still do it.

The interaction of several motivations is well illustrated by Valeska, who combines a desire to leave Poland with a plan to earn money and learn English while seeking adventure:

So I wanted to, to change my life and try something new, learn something new. So it was like a challenge, adventure, a possibility to earn money to, to learn English language and it is my hobby to learn English.

This interaction of different reasons is not uncommon and reflects the complexity of the reality of decision making.

The desire and expectation of earning "good money" in the UK was mentioned by all but five of the interviewees, often in conjunction with other reasons. For four of them, the possibility of earning money served as a pull factor in stark contrast to their current financial situation, in which they felt that they were not adequately rewarded for the work that they were doing.

Edmund, for example, who was a qualified IT specialist in Poland, was unable to find IT-related employment in his region and had to work some 250 miles away in Warsaw. Although he did not object too much to having to travel so far to find work, and although he felt that the money was "decent", he was not happy with the demands of the job:

I just stopped fancying working fifteen hours a day for quite a decent salary. I just prefer working eight hours a day for a decent salary, so the only country that can give me that and the only country I can assimilate to is England because I know English.

Cecylja, who found it easy to obtain work as a specialised secretary in Poland and was very happy in her work there, nevertheless struggled financially:

When I worked in Poland I just earned some money and I have to spend that money for all bills, for mortgage for my flat and then I don't have any money for anything. So that was the problem.

As a trained doctor, with some twenty-five years' experience of working in a first aid medical station, Brigita felt that she could do better financially. The situation was made worse for her as a result of her husband's lengthy illness and subsequent hip replacement operation. She was very hopeful of eventually being able to earn more money in the UK once she had completed her conversion course, which she combined with a job in a care home:

..it is very important for me this financial side, because in Lithuania I was upset about it and I'm not absolutely happy at the moment, but hopefully in future situation will improve, more or less.

Veronika, unlike Brigita, had difficulty in finding work in Latvia in her specialised legal field after graduating. Although she realised that she would earn more as she gained more experience, she did not feel motivated, since:

... working in Latvia I would earn ... as erm a specialist in law for businesses ... about two hundred, two hundred and fifty pound a month, so it wasn't really enough ... I knew that working on a farm here I can earn more money.

The reason that Veronika knew that she could earn more in the UK was because whilst at university she had spent some time here picking strawberries on a Student Exchange Programme. This shows the complexity of the decision making process as a series of factors - lack of well-paid work at home (push factor); possibility of earning more money in the UK (pull factor) and previous time spent working in the UK (prior contact) - combined to help her to reach the decision to come.

If those who had work in their home country felt a need to migrate in order to earn more, then it is perhaps not a surprise to learn that three of the interviewees felt a need for money as a result of being unemployed in their home country. For them, the prospect of finding work and being adequately rewarded for it was a strong motivating factor.

Jiri, who had lost his job as a pathologist in his mid 50's some three months prior to moving to the UK, felt a strong need to find employment. Even though the work he was doing in a warehouse was very demanding on him physically, he felt compensated since:

... I am now paid ... almost the same ... working here as a warehouse worker ... like a pathologist in my country. ... It was the only move which I was, er, able to do because ... from the 1st August I was unemployed and I have came to UK the 8th of November.

The stigma of unemployment in Poland weighed heavily on Valeska. Somewhat paradoxically, she was determined to save money in order to return to Poland and not have to work. Here again, the desire for money was mixed up with other factors, not least of which was a desire to boost her self esteem.

Now I work as a slave but for money I can save for not working in future. Good solution for me. But when you have no work you are treating in your environment as .. outcast without respect.

Sofija's desire for a steady income was also a factor in her decision to come. Being unable to find regular employment after being made redundant, she was perhaps not fully aware of the relative cost of living between Latvia and the UK:

when I get my first wage, 200 pound, I thought Oh God, what I'm going to do with such big money?".. previously I get 80 pound per month.

The remaining interviewees who mentioned money either had clear financial needs as a result of financial obligations which they had had difficulty in meeting or were attempting to use their time here to pre-fund a future course of action. For some, such as Stanislaw and Andrzej, the need for money was acute, leaving them little choice but to raise funds quickly:

My mother fought against the cancer, yes, so the treatment was erm very expensive so we er I mean we family we ran out of money so I had to go abroad and earn some money (Stanislaw)

I was problem, financial problem in Poland ..I take credit, er.. erm.. I have to out from Poland (Andrzej).

For others, the possibility of an enhanced income was seen as an opportunity to finance a planned ongoing commitment, serving as a motivator to stay here:

My course costs more than three thousand a year - I need money for study (Isabella).

In Brazil ... we wanted our own, our property. And so if we live here around three years, we can get this property .... We already bought it, and we finish in around [speaking together] one year and a half more (Juliana & Ricardo).

I must get money for my next study... Simple reason ...... and you make this money and it's the, for example half year .. without any meaning in your life ... but you have money and you can develop yourself or, you know, in the next level. For example for me would be a study in Amsterdam. (Sebastian).

Fourteen of the nineteen interviewees mentioned money as a motivating factor. However, the financial reasons given by the interviewees varied. In some cases, (Andrzej, Stanislaw) there was an urgent need for money due to debts or family pressure, in others (Sebastian, Isabella, Juliana, Ricardo) a desire to accumulate funds to sponsor ongoing or future studies or investments, in other cases (Edmund, Veronika) a desire to earn enough to be comfortable, without having to work long hours or a desire simply to be able to work at all and earn a living (Brigita, Cecylja, Jiri, Ona, Sofija, Valeska).

Another common motivator behind the decision to come to the UK was a desire to improve one's education. Six interviewees cited the opportunity to study as a motivating factor in coming to the UK. Gabriela, who had served an internship in the United Nations in Rio and was intending to enrol on a postgraduate degree in International Security in Leicester University, saw the concept of self development - of "growing" - as a major attraction of coming to the UK, and one which she felt was shared by others:

I think many people here, other migrants, workers, they are coming here because in their country they don't have opportunity to grow.

This sense of freedom to "grow" took different forms for different interviewees. For some, it meant a chance to become more proficient in the English language, for others the opportunity to improve their CV by taking vocational courses, and for others still the chance to pursue tertiary study. All of these things could have been achieved without leaving the home country but with more difficulty and at a higher cost:

I cannot learn English when I work in Poland and you know, go to the classes with the Polish people and that's it (Cecylja).

I did study English in school and er unfortunately, the teacher, she didn't speak the language, so she couldn't teach us to speak the language so I could read and understand (Veronika).

Here, I have my books, the Internet, I can study and have enough money (Isabella).

[In Holland] I wanted to carry on my education, but the cost was high because I wasn't on, on government [support]. The moment I got job, everything can't [his eligibility for support ceased]. So, it is still in my mind to carry on my education here as well (Kamal).

Those who wanted to study English cited the relatively high cost of studying English in the home country - when compared with the chance to enrol on free or very cheap EFL (English as a Foreign Language) classes in the UK - as a major attraction in coming here:

... I can learn English language I .. have benefits from this, no, but I like this, it's like a hobby, no? I can read very interesting things so it enrich my life. I .. this is big issue, big issue. (Valeska)

Gabriela, who had converted to Islam in Brazil, was also studying Arabic for beginners and found this highly motivating:

in Brazil, never I could learn [Arabic]. There is very expensive, only got private lessons there. Can't develop. Here, I go every Saturday. I walk twenty minutes, to the Community College, Leicester. It's really easy.

As well as a desire to improve their own education, two of the four interviewees whose children were with them in the UK were motivated by the chance to improve their children's education.

Brigita, whose eldest son (23) was married and settled back in Lithuania, had been joined by her twenty-year-old son and fifteen-year-old daughter, both of whom were doing very well at school, with the son applying for a university place and the daughter being accepted to study the violin at Birmingham Conservatoire:

er.. it's about my children. They have more possibilities to get er proper education and to go to the UK diploma, not like mine ... ... just because of my family now I decided to do it.

Gabriela's children were much younger (10 years, 4 years and 9 months) and much of the attraction for her in their being here was their exposure to an Islamic environment and also the opportunity for them to learn English:

So I think also, you see also about the consequence of the future, I think this period for my children would be very good for them.

Push factors

Several push factors were mentioned by respondents as shaping their decision to leave their respective countries. These factors should be viewed as operating in conjunction with one another and with one or more pull factors as part of a complex decision-making process.

One factor mentioned by five of the interviewees was the lack of work opportunities in the home country. The decision to come to the UK was motivated in part by a desire to escape from redundancy or continued periods of unemployment. For three of the interviewees, the decision was taken when they were between University and a job:

Veronika's inability to find work in Latvia was as a result of her lack of experience, as she had only just graduated:

I've tried to find some job in Latvia but ... because it's, it was a high unemployment in Latvia, so everybody wasn't just interested in qualifications, they were interested in experience. I didn't have experience, so I didn't have chance to get really anything.

Similarly, Celine decided to move to the UK immediately after graduating from her Master's degree in Geography and Cartography, justifying her decision on the basis that :

I had nothing to lose in France, I had just finished my qualification, didn't get a job straight away.

Another decision taken between study and work was taken by Gabriela:
Yeah, when I come here I was not working. I had finished the United Nations. I was only studying, I was finishing my course. So I finished, I had finished all the disciplines, I was starting to write my, my small essay for finish the course.

For this group of interviewees, then, the ending of their studies seemed an ideal time to take the plunge and the move to the UK seemed preferable to an extended job search in their home countries.

In contrast, Jiri, who was in his mid 50's when he lost his job as a pathologist in the Czech Republic, had spent his whole life in the same field and was at a loss as to what work he could find, other than occasional unregistered, untaxed jobs:
I've lost my job in August er 2005 .. from the 1st August I was unemployed and I have came to UK the 8th of November… I have been working in, in the black way, yes? At about two months, then I was waiting for the going away because we have bought the ticket.

A similar frustration was felt by Valeska, who found it increasingly difficult to obtain work:
I found myself in .. a blind alley, yeah? Without work and I didn't work for five years. It was, it were only occasionally jobs as .. care for people with Alzheimer's disease. I found very, very difficult to have job.

Dissatisfaction with the work situation was cited as a reason for leaving the home country by five of the interviewees:
For Ona, the inability to find a job commensurate with her qualifications was a motivating factor in her decision to leave, as she felt that if she were to do such work, it might as well be in the UK where she would earn more for it:
I couldn't do my job .. I'm qualified lab assistant. I couldn't find a job in there as a lab assistant so I had to work simple work like in a hardware store, I used to work in a hardware store, .. my last job before I came here, so basically not exactly what I [laughs] trained to be, and that's why I came to the UK .

For Sofija, the impermanency of her job helped her to decide to move to the UK:
I left that job because it wasn't long term, it was just for a couple of months. It wasn't like tabled, you know, like really definitely I can have it … it was temporary work. They couldn't promise me that I'm going to

get it, like.

Edmund, who had to take up work some 250 miles from his hometown, was frustrated at the number of hours he had to work in order to make a decent salary:

I could find probably a job .. in Warsaw again .. I would have to work about fiftee, sixteen hours a day just to get a very decent salary.

The sense of dissatisfaction with the current job extended to those who were working in other countries. This was the case for Juliana and Ricardo who had left Brazil for a job in Germany but soon became disillusioned at working sixteen-hour days and decided to come to the UK after hearing from friends that working life in the UK was less stressful.

In four cases, interviewees reported less specific feelings of unease with life in their home country, which played a role in their decision to migrate.

Celine eloquently expressed her malaise with life in France some fifteen years previously, when she decided to come to England as an au pair on a "kind of a gap year really":

There was another reason why I left France, which was sort of.. personal. I was a little bit fed up with France. I had, I had done a lot of studies and if I thought, you know, it's climbing a mountain when you're at the top for years when I've got this qualification [Master's degree in Geography and Cartography] to be like a nice, green and pleasant land beyond this mountain and then reaching the top, I realised no, it isn't. It's just the same, more of the same. There wasn't this nice green paradise behind it, it was the same. So I was a bit fed up with .. I can't explain, it's difficult to say. I was just, I was not terribly happy.

Brigita lays the blame for the disillusionment her family felt on the general economic and political climate in Lithuania:

It was like automatically, you know, my son finished from school, my husband recovered from operation, and he has no future in Lithuania as well, he said. He can see no future for himself, for me and for the family. Because of big corruption, you know, everywhere in Lithuania ... and we decided start from the beginning here in UK.

Similarly, Isabella felt frustrated with the general economy in Portugal:
Because my country is not a good country. It's a poor country ...economy in my country is down...

For Kamal, whose initial migration to Holland from Iran was on the basis of political asylum, the disillusionment was not with the home country, but with the lifestyle in Holland, which he found rather boring and devoid of opportunity for interesting activities:

I, I didn't find it [Holland] very stimulating country. ..... There was no much more to do and I didn't, I'm not that kind of person to come to do the job and go home. ... I could see, ... thirty years later on, .. I'm on my pension and ... I didn't want that, I want more, be more active.

Ties and links with the UK

Aside from the factors which attracted the migrants to the UK or exerted an influence on them to leave their home countries, their willingness to uproot themselves and start an adventure in the UK seemed to vary based on their previous travel experiences and their access to a network of family and friends already in the UK.

Three interviewees took advice from friends in the UK before deciding to come here and four interviewees cited the fact that they had family members who were living or had lived in the UK as an influencing factor in their decision to move here. Of note is the consistent implication that these family members exerted pressure on them to come:

and the other .. cause was my sister. She always been here ... we were just speaking on the phone. I said 'Well, I just given notice to my employer' and she said 'Well, OK so you have a ticket .. to England and I said 'wh- what for?' 'Well, you can work here. So right if you can call it an invitation, yes that was an invitation. I was actually placed by the wall and 'there's your ticket man c'mon' [chuckles] (Edmund).

The implication that the sister was press-ganging Edmund to come is echoed to some extent in Jiri's droll suggestion that he was dictated to by his daughter:

The reason was .. that it was in the same year in er vacancy [holidays] from school er my daughter here for two months. It was in July and August. She was also earning here money .. and my daughter said me that 'come to England' so I have been going to England [laughs].

Throughout Kamal's interview, frequent mention is made of pressure by the wife, through her family, for Kamal to leave his secure post with MSF in Holland and move to an uncertain future in the UK:

For my wife .. her brother, her family live here. So .. she really felt down. There was no, I mean, family member around. ..... I said 'Listen, ... we are not going to get the job we have. .. But, if you're not happy, so it affects me, it affects both of us and our life. And in a way she pursue me,' Let's try.

Sofija had agreed to accompany her then boyfriend to Spalding to stay with his aunt. This facilitated their first few weeks in the UK:

It actually was my ex-boyfriend who asked me to come with him because he had some family member here already so he said 'OK, we can try something and see how it's going to be.' His aunt promised a job for me and him and promised a place for the first time we could stay.

After the relationship broke down, Sofija decided to stay on and moved into a house with several people from a range of countries, so that she would be forced to use English to communicate with them.

For three others, recommendations and assistance from friends in the UK was influential in their decision. Juliana and Ricardo were persuaded by friends in Boston that working in the UK was considerably less demanding than working in Germany, where they had both been putting in fiteen to sixteen hours a day in an ice cream shop. The ties between migrants even extended within the sample:

... and second thing is my mate [Stanislaw]. He lives here and uh, he told me that I can come. We are from the same city in, in, in Poland. er.. when he.. leave Poland and start to work in UK, ... we have still contact with ... each other and, I told him that I need a money and, for my study and he say 'you can come to UK and, and get some job and get some money. Simple' (Sebastian).

Previous visits to the UK

Pawel and Gabriela had both originally come to the UK for a brief visit, without the intention of seeking work. Both subsequently decided to stay on and take up a job. Similarly, Edmund, whose sister, a long term UK resident, had been instrumental in persuading him to visit her and investigate the possibility of working here, subsequently decided to stay for longer and look for an even better job:

I know that many Polish people did go to London and see what happens. I've never had that on my mind. I just came over here .. found job. Yeah why not? I might stay here."

Three others - Stanislaw, Celine and Veronika - reminisced about previous trips to England and pointed out that these trips had made their decision to move here easier. Despite this, their positive perception of the time they had spent here clearly played a role in influencing them to return here:

it's not like I spent all my life in Poland and er I was, you know, dropped in deep water, cos er I was in England in er 1999 and I spent a week in

London with my English friend, an Englishman who moved to Poland ... so he needs a van, I had it, so he asked me to go with him to London, spend a week in his house and go back with some stuff - furniture, things like that (Stanislaw).

England was an obvious choice really because I had liked meeting English people in France and I thought they were very nice people and I had good memories of coming to England in year nine, when I was fourteen, I think, for an exchange, you know, a linguistic exchange with my pen-friend. (Celine)

I think 2001 is the first time when I came over ... on a Student Exchange Programme first for half a year at first. So I was picking strawberries in the farm, near Southampton - Beaulieu area, New Forest Area. After that ... we're going home and finish University. (Veronika)

Previous visits to other countries

In addition, comments made by three of the interviewees indicated that previous time spent abroad, not just in the UK, was a factor which increased their propensity to move:

During Kamal's ten years in Holland he had been granted political asylum and Dutch nationality, studied IT and the Dutch language intensively, and found a job as a Network Administrator with Médecins Sans Frontières. These experiences largely dispelled any fear in seeking work in the UK:

We have right of work, we have right to a study. So it's a matter of finding a job.

Stanislaw felt that his travels in Europe would stand him in good stead for his time in the UK. By pointing out that he had avoided registering with the authorities in Holland, he implied a sense of confidence in his ability to cope with any demands of working here:

and one year later I went to Norway to visit my ex-girlfriend and I spent a few weeks just wandering across the country from the south to the north and I was travelling to other eastern European countries like Czechoslovakia, Eastern Germany, Ukraine, Latvia, Estonia ... and one year before I came to England in 2004 I spent three months in Netherlands working illegally.

This air of self-assurance as a result of previous time spent working outside of the home country was shared by Isabella:

But I'm, I'm one person, adaptation in the life ... I stay one time in

Belgium, working in airport, I working in the airport do sales, you know … and then I finish my money for finish my course, for this important, for my course. But, I'm adaptation for any country, me.

An understanding of the migrants' motivations in coming to the UK is central to this study. These are demand-pull factors, both financial and other, which attracted them to the UK; supply-push factors, such as unemployment in the home country; and the existence of networks of compatriots, family and friends in the UK.

Freedom of movement
The freedom of movement granted the interviewees under the EU Accession treaty made it possible for the A8 interviewees to seek work in Britain, Ireland and Sweden without committing themselves. However, those interviewees with citizenship from the older member countries of the EU had no such restrictions. Of the six interviewees in this category, only Celine and Isabella were indigenous Europeans (French and Portuguese respectively). The others, - Juliana and Ricardo (Brazilians with Italian passports); Kamal (Iranian granted Dutch nationality in 2000); and Gabriela (Brazilian with a Portuguese passport) – were able to use their secondary nationality to benefit from full EU rights. This enabled them to move freely between countries.

Before leaving Brazil, Juliana and Ricardo had ignored their friends' advice to turn down a job offer from Germany and work in the UK instead. They soon regretted their decision. However, as EU citizens, they were able to leave Germany and come to work in the UK in a very short space of time:

[Our friends in the UK said on the phone] ".. good money, better than in Germany. If you want to come, you can come, no problem … we can help you" .. The first flight we took it straight.

The freedom of movement the interviewees enjoy is in sharp contrast to the "go or stay" decisions historically faced by migrants such as Mexicans migrating to the United States, and underlines the important distinction between migration and mobility. The knowledge that they would be able to return to their normal environment without bringing about any permanent changes clearly had an impact on the migrants' decision to come.

Brigita, having spent twenty-five years working for the same employers in her hometown, was careful to ensure that she would not be making a permanent break from them:

I know any time I can go back. Yeah. I asked my colleagues and my er [laughs] employers. "Can I go back?", "yeah" they said, "anytime".

The ease with which these migrants were able to enter and leave the UK and the relative lack of expense involved in such comings and goings clearly played a role in allowing them to come here in the first place. Additionally, it made it possible for them to go back to their home country easily in the event of a family emergency. Those with spouses back home were able to return on a visit or be visited here without bureaucratic or financial hurdles. Such considerations may have played a part in persuading them to come here.

Although all of the interviewees in this study had made the decision to stay on after an initial visit, the possibility of abandoning the plan to stay and work in the UK and returning to one's own country was also very real. This was evidenced by their accounts of friends who had not stayed on. Ironically, in some cases the interviewees had only reluctantly agreed to accompany a friend to the UK, whereas the now long-departed friend had been determined to make a new life here. Pawel had arrived with a friend who was very keen to settle in the UK whereas Pawel himself was uncommitted. She, however, had left six months after arriving. Sofija had been persuaded by her then boyfriend to come along and stay with his aunt. He left soon afterwards. Such accounts illustrate that the decision to remain in the UK was one which could vary from individual to individual and which could evolve against their expectations.

Having addressed the question of why they chose to come to the UK initially, we now look at the techniques they employed in order to find work here.

Initial job search

From the interviewees' accounts, a clear distinction emerged between those who left for the UK with a job already arranged and those who decided to look for a job after arriving.

Of those arriving with a job arranged, four had a job contract arranged through an agency in their home country, and two had arranged their job by themselves. Of those arriving without a job arranged, four arrived on a speculative visit, either finding and taking up a job quickly, or arranging one, then returning to the home country to finalise their move; seven stayed with friends or family whilst looking for a job, and one joined her spouse after he had found work and she had completed her studies

The interviewees using a home country agency were content to allow the agencies to advise them as to the nature and location of work available. In particular, they placed little or no importance on the location of the work the agencies could offer them:

I just came here from work agency, straight to Leicester, they got a job here. So that's why. I'm not, not thinking. I just said, 'OK I'm going', I

want to go to England, but it doesn't matter where. (Cecylja)

Because, I got an offer from Polish job agency, which recruited, was recruiting, Polish people for a care assistant job in Britain ... I got two offers, from two different companies and I had problem to choose. But, I got free ticket, plane ticket, so I erm, choose this offer. (Valeska)

You just have to go there and work .. it doesn't matter where .. I came through the agency .. I've been promised work in the onion fields (Ona).

This lack of attention to their destination region manifested itself later, once the interviewees had come to know the characteristics of the area where they were working. Ona, for example, was surprised to find that West Bromwich was not a rural oasis, and Cecylja was taken totally aback by the proportion of non-white residents in Leicester:

It's so completely opposite of my imagination of it ... basically .. From outside, UK looks so ... great, so different .. but when you come here .. I don't know, the environment and the people over here ... when I came here .. I was really shocked (Ona).

I was surprised when I see so many people from other countries, from India, especially here. (Cecylja)

Both Ona and Cecylja went on to make comments about the ethnic minorities in their cities which could be described as racist. Such comments were more widespread throughout the sample.

Location did not seem to be such an important issue for the interviewees after arrival. Though many changed jobs, once they had found work, they stayed within the same geographical area, except for Stanislaw whose move was arranged through his ongoing agency agreement, and Ona, who walked out of a job in the onion fields of Lincolnshire to seek work in a more industrial area.

Both Isabella and Celine were able to arrange jobs on their own without recourse to an agency. In Celine's case, this was relatively straightforward, since she had access to specialized media advertisements from English families looking for au pairs. Isabella took great trouble to make sure that the job she saw advertised in a Road Chef would be suitable, making enquiries about safety issues when working at night, before making up her mind to come.

Thirteen of the nineteen interviewees, however, took advantage of the freedom of movement within the EU which allowed them to visit the UK with the intention of trying to find work after arrival:

... let's try. We are not going to go through a violent procedure because we are EU citizen anyway. (Kamal)

Such a decision was made even easier if a close friend or a family member was already in the UK and able to assist in the search for a job. However, it was also taken even in the absence of such a contact.

Five interviewees arrived in the UK without any network of friends or family here to assist them in their initial job search. This put extra financial pressure on them to find a job before their funds ran out. A further seven stayed with friends or relatives, which alleviated the financial pressure on them somewhat. Marjanna joined her husband Edmund after about six months and started to seek work also.

Whether through financial pressure or a simple desire to work, many of these thirteen interviewees wasted no time in finding jobs, with the help of agencies:

But I just came over here, went to some agencies and I didn't know this is so easy to get a job in this country. (Edmund)

I just came here and, was, for example, Thursday and on the Friday, the next day, I have a job. (Sebastian)

OK I arrived here on March and I started looking for a job to the agency as well and I found .. a job er .. in a warehouse, it was something with clothes, very simple work (Marjanna).

[Finding a job was] very simple. These two, .. from .. acquaintance with my daughter which I have mentioned before, so er they led me to the agency. We were in two agencies (Jiri).

I found it [a job as a care assistant] immediately (Brigita).

Others took longer to find a job. Andrzej, who had very little English on arrival and was intent, as a vet, on working with animals, took around a month until he successfully applied for a job as an animal technician in a laboratory. Kamal was equally intent on finding work within his specialism, IT, but was unsuccessful and finally took on work in a chicken factory, though not without trying hard to find an IT post:

When I came here in 2004, for three weeks I sent more than 43 application forms.

Pawel, who put off actively seeking work until he had decided whether or not to stay, also took several weeks to start work.

Overall, there seemed to be little trouble in finding a job, either alone or through an agency, if the interviewees were willing to take on jobs for which they were overqualified, whereas jobs which were more in keeping with their background were harder to find. Some resentment was felt towards agencies:

they were never looking into my CV properly .. they're not reading my CV and trying to make a laugh of me ... asking me ... 'Can you use a computer?''Well, I said 'That's what it says on my CV over there you're handling."(Edmund)

I knew from the start that the agencies, are, it's best to avoid working through an agency, so that's why ... through the other people's experience ... so that's why I avoided it all the way. I never worked for an agency. Never, in England. (Veronika)

Later, here in UK, I have maybe three agencies working for me, I applied for them, and again the same situation. They sometimes offer 'Can I send your CV to this place, this place?''and later... nothing happened (Brigita)

An examination of the migrants' motives in seeking work in the UK revealed a mixture of pull factors, push factors, and the influence of existing networks of friends and family members already in the UK. These should not be considered as existing in isolation. Rather, the complexity of the decision-making process meant that these factors interacted in complicated ways.

Among the pull factors which attracted the migrants to the UK were a sense of adventure, the lure of "good money", an opportunity to clear off debt or address an urgent financial need, and the possibility of educational advancement for oneself and/or one's children. The push factors consisted of an inability to find work in the home country, dissatisfaction with the current job, and disillusionment with the home country. The existence of a network of family members and/or friends in the UK played a part in persuading some migrants to come, as did fond memories of previous visits to the UK or to other countries. The freedom of movement granted to European Union citizens was an important factor in persuading the migrants to seek work in the UK, since it left them the option of returning home at any time.

Chapter 5: Barriers in finding work commensurate with qualifications and experience

In contrast with those who quickly obtained menial employment, those who had been independently job hunting in the hope of finding more suitable work soon realised that jobs more commensurate with their qualifications and experience were extremely hard to come by.

Brigita, who had been reliably informed by a friend working as a doctor in the UK and an agency in her hometown that she should be able to find professional work in the medical field, soon discovered that this was not the case:

I applied thousand times maybe. I applied by post and er I sent these application forms and er online and .. nothing no reply. Sometimes they sent me letters Thank you for applying. Sorry you were not selected. Try again. Like this.

Kamal was reluctant to take on work below his level, having found a very good job in Holland but experiencing intense pressure from his wife to move nearer to her family in the UK. He too, encountered difficulties in finding a post:

First, first I tried my level, network administration, because I had the fresh experience ... I had only one reply, I remember, in city centre. They wanted Lotus Notes administrator. Was perfect for me. I've done this ... I was really happy ... I turned up to the interview ... Fifty minutes I was waiting, there was a reception and the guy came in a suit and said "Well yes, sorry, we don't need to do the interview." I said, "What's the reason?" He said "We already pick up somebody else."

Andrzej placed a free classified ad advertising his services as a vet to the Polish community, which brought a modicum of short-term success:

Polish newspapers print my er you know I am a vet I looking for the job" er for free, two weeks .. er .. from this message there was two veterinary visits in London [laughs] yeah, because I from Poland .. take every veterinary tools - stethoscope and every hand tools - because I'm surgeon specialist. I have two visits in London, .. Polish people.

The need for good English

The applicants themselves were very aware that their real or perceived lack of English was a reason for the failure of these job applications. All interviewees were very aware of their own level of English language ability. Their ability to cope in English, and their level of confidence in this ability, played a key role in helping to form their expectations as to the prospects they faced.

The interviewees can be placed into three broad groups according to their ability in English:

The first group claimed to have an almost total lack of English on arrival:

I could say what my name is and where I come from, that is all what I could say (Sofija).

When I come to England my English is zero, zero – only "Good morning" and "F*** off" (Andrzej).

They also faced the realisation that this lack of command of the language would seriously impair their freedom of choice in the job market. Andrzej, in his search for a position in a veterinary clinic, found that his minimal knowledge of English was a major handicap:

"I looking job in every veterinary clinic around maybe [laughs] a hundred mile. ... I going for every clinic the same problem. 'Sorry. Your qualification's very good, very nice but your English is not good.' ... I have qualification ... I can make every operation but I can't talking with English people because it's very special talk".

Juliana, who was a journalist in Brazil, was acutely aware of the gap in her knowledge of the language and knew that she would not be able to carry out such work in the UK:

I know, I can't work like a journalist here .. impossible, impossible! If I study English and I improve my English, my .. listening maybe ... but now is impossible.

For the second group, the aim was to improve their command of the English language in order to gain access to better jobs, or to vocational or tertiary courses in the UK. The role of the IELTS exam was central to the latter as it is required for admission onto tertiary level courses in the UK.

Gabriela had had difficulty in finding an IELTS preparation course in Brazil and was attracted by the possibility of attending such a course here in order to meet the requirements for enrolment on a postgraduate degree in International Relations. Kamal saw the offer of funding for an IELTS course by his employer as a potential means of improving his job prospects and making him a better candidate in the eyes of potential employers.

This group were willing to take on menial jobs as long as they could also study English in order to enable them to consider more suitable jobs:

after being for here a year and a half I .. decided I really want to learn the language and er want to do something, you know, better than, you know, what I was doing. Then the money is .. no longer was of interest to me. I thought I'd better, you know, sort of get a better education and, you know, do something better. So I went to Peterborough College. I was working and going in the evening classes to Peterborough College studying English there er and then going to Boston College ... to different places and it was all about English (Veronika).

English Language training had the added advantage of being inexpensive or free.

in Brazil, never I could learn, there is very expensive, only got private lessons there. Can't develop. Here, I go every Saturday, I walk twenty minutes, to the Community College, Leicester. It's really easy, cheap (Gabriela).

in Poland I can go English classes, but I don't have money for that, so I just try to learn myself and I listen to programs on TV or something like that and then that's it but here I can afford classes easy (Cecylja).

However, attendance on such courses was often difficult to arrange as a result of shift work or irregular working hours:

I have been in four, I think four colleges and I was rejected every time because .. I have er changeable shifts morning shift and the second week is the er afternoon shift. That it is colliding and I er it was about er half an hour that I would have to go, half an hour in two weeks er earlier, and I was told it was not possible - that I have not to go for, for the English classes (Jiri).

I'm, I'm (sneaking out) about, because there's ... this program I must going there, you know, strictly, it's not possible to working in afternoon shifts and going and teaching, learning in program, yeah? (Sebastian)

I was working, it was very difficult for me, because, this course was at morning and I started .. afternoon shift at 2 o'clock so when I got up, I go to course and after course home and for, for preparation to work and when I get from work it was after 11 (Valeska).

67

The members of the third group **Error! Reference source not found.**were fluent in English on arrival. Indeed, both Celine and Pawel used their fluency in the language as a source of income, by taking on part time interpreting and translating work. Celine had found some translation work through an agency after being made redundant

I enjoyed it [the interpreting] a lot yes. In fact I was surviving doing that job. But, it was on a on-call basis. (Celine).

I used to do some interpreting as well, for courts, for Police, for lots of these (Pawel).

They felt confident that, even if they were unable to find suitable work, they would be able to enrol on vocational training courses leading to such work.

I must train myself, I keep myself updated, ... I have online this er BNG Learning and I do this modules, they send some modules to my email and I try to do it, just to memorise everything, you know to be in touch with Medicine.... And er as a care assistant I attend different courses as well (Brigita).

Non-recognition of qualifications and experience
The interviewees encountered a scepticism on the part of potential employers and agencies with respect to the value of foreign qualifications:

Sometimes potential employers look at my diploma ℰr it's not our diploma, it's not our accent"[laughs] (Brigita).

In Poland you have to know a lot of different er kinds of accountancies, different kinds of documents to, to do something, yeah, but here is just very simple work, but nobody wants to give me that chance to learn it (Marjanna).

when some .. employer, who see the, some Polish guy finish a Polish school, it's nothing for them, I think, yeah? (Sebastian).

The insistence on UK experience expressed by potential employers and agencies proved highly frustrating for the interviewees. Marjanna, freshly qualified as an accountant in Poland, joined her husband Edmund in the UK only to find that her brand new degree was of little use to her in finding work in her field:

Do you have any experience in England?"No," I say "not any but I have experience in Poland, yes?"No, no, no if you have no any experience in England, you can't start doing something better, yeah."

Her husband Edmund encountered a similar difficulty when trying to find work in his specialised field of IT, and became somewhat aggrieved at the attitude he encountered in employment agencies:

That was my problem to find an IT job in here. Do you have any experience in England?"No, I don't I came, just came to this country."Well, sorry, you will have to have at least two years' experience to do something."Well, that's what I did for about ten years in Poland, how is it different from the one you have in this country? The different language only of using, of people using it, nothing else. I mean how is it a different computer in this country than ... in Poland?

Pawel, who was a teacher in Poland, tried to find a job in education. He too was told that he lacked UK experience and found the red tape involved too much to handle:

I wanted to come here and I would be a teacher ... but I literally, I couldn't, it was impossible to have all these documents. There were two or three things, it was impossible for me to have that and it was probably something ... about experience ... of teaching in the UK ... it was like vicious circle, I couldn't, so I couldn't go out of it.

Financial pressures

Whether they had been offered posts prior to leaving for the UK or had arrived intending to find a job, the interviewees were faced with the economic need to find work as soon as possible in order to survive:

I walking every day walking to er .. job centre and er all London walking because when I start I was only 300 pound er travelling in London is very expensive I walking and when I find job in job centre I go to er Internet Cafe and send my CV to .. find this job by Internet. (Andrzej).

In such cases, sooner or later, the financial pressures of surviving in the UK were such that the interviewees required a job – any job – in order not to have to return home. Faced with the need for money, they took on jobs which they knew to be below their level, often on a short-term contract.

Pawel decided to take on physical work with a garden designer, a type of work which he had never done before, purely out of financial need:

I had no choice .. because of a simple thing, which is money I needed. I wanted to stay here, I didn't want to come back at that point, I still wanted to stay here. One of my best friends was here and we supported each other,

I would say. And she was doing the job she didn't like as well so, I .. I just not have choice because we needed money for rent to live and things like this, .. and we had no savings at this time.

Kamal, whose last post was as a network administrator, eventually tired of applying for jobs in IT and approached the local Job Centre for a job as quality controller in a chicken factory, a job he felt he had to take on out of financial need:

He saw my CV [laughs] and said, I don't know who sent you here, you are too overqualified for this job. I don't know what we can do. But, if this is what you want, it's perfect by me, so why not? I said OK, I took the job. I have to pay the bills anyway. I can't stay with my friends. I took the job.

The need to earn money frequently manifested itself in willingness to take on part time or temporary posts on an ad hoc basis from agencies. After working for some time in such jobs, the desire for a permanent post often outweighed the desire for a more suitable job.

.. agency found me some one, two week job and I was just taking any assignment I can get: one, two day .. just to get er some money .. because obviously I was starving in this country (Edmund).

it wasn't a permanent job, I was working like two days a week, three days a week, sometimes five days a week, sometimes a day a week. Sometimes five hours a day, sometimes seven hours a day (Pawel).

So, in this warehouse as well they have not every day job (Valeska).

I started in one agency, but it wasn't quite good, I had job maybe two or three times a week, it wasn't enough (Sofija).

So they said me about.. they said about 3, 4 months that job, it will be (Cecylja).

In ascertaining the barriers which prevented the migrants from obtaining jobs commensurate with their qualifications and skills, the main reasons identified were a lack of English language skills, a reluctance on the part of agencies and potential employers to recognise non-UK qualifications and experience, and a lack of funds sufficient to finance a long job search.

Chapter 6: Coping with the skill- and status-underemployment

A sense of surprise became apparent once a menial job was undertaken. The migrants had to come to terms with five changes: the physical nature of the work; the repetitive nature of the work; the stressful working environment; relationships with co-workers; and their own social perceptions in the eyes of others.

Demanding work environments

The physical nature of the work soon took its toll on those who were previously unaccustomed to manual labour:

Pawel, having spent most of his savings and not having obtained a teaching post, decided reluctantly to take on a job working with a garden designer, doing work with his hands, something he was not accustomed to:

I just didn't like the feeling of going there at all. Actually, I hated it and I was moaning to others that my fingers will be damaged and you know, like, stuff like this. So I, I didn't like doing that at all ..... it was hell like.

Jiri, who was in his mid fifties and had failing eyesight, found the demanding nature of his job, which required him to place almost two hundred palettes an hour, some heavy, into one of thirty-two cages, extremely tiring at first:

So in this warehouse for me is difficult work ... maybe not now after two years but .... working there after morning shift I am so tired I must to go to the bed for one hour and a half, two hours to sleep and to be able to read. I'm not able after this shift er reading ... Every day, even now, I have aches in my muscles yeah, of the hands, of the arms ...

Valeska, who was also over 50 years of age, found it very hard mentally and physically to do her factory job :

Eight hours. On my legs ... All day, the same thing, again and again. Like robot.

Cecylja, who had suffered a bad back injury when a swimming instructor in Poland, found difficulty in meeting the physical demands of her job:

About the warehouse operating? Yeah. It was different because in Poland, just like you know, I'm reading all the time and just use my brain and here was like a physical, you know. And, it was different, I was surprised that I can manage this. Because I was really afraid that I cannot doing this, because it is a difficult job, I've got problem with my back and it was feel weak.

A further challenge was the difficulty in relating to repetitive, simple work. Gabriela, who had been a veterinary surgeon and worked for the UN was much unfulfilled in her administrative job:

It's small company. They have five petrol stations, but it's not a big company. So it's boring. I don't like. It's like automatic job, it's very below what I can do.

Valeska, who had been out of work for five years before coming to the UK, had great difficulty in relating to the kind of work she was doing, seeing it as worthless and degrading:

it was very hard work for me. But, sometimes .. I was not engaged, I was never engaged in this job, like other women. And it was visible, I think.

Juliana and Ricardo, whose previous work in Germany had been very demanding but involved them in interactions with customers, found their jobs in a pizza factory less physically demanding but very much lacking in mental stimulation:

..it's very boring. We are losing our mind ...we don't need to use the mind, it's automatically, like a machine .. and every day is the same.

Another shock was felt when coming to terms with the everyday stress of hectic working life. Kamal, whose previous work had been as a psychologist in his native Iran and then a network administrator in Holland, was ill prepared for the stress of his job as a quality controller in a chicken factory:

I lost almost nine kilogram the first six months ..... Shouting, the harassment, the bullying, the payment, the way they treating people. I couldn't believe it. ... And two times I've been .. bullied by my manager. First time I stopped it and second time I've been attacked by engineer with [laughs] a screwdriver.

Jiri, who had been made redundant in the Czech Republic, expressed fear of losing his job here, which he had held since arriving in the UK. He was concerned that at his age he would find it difficult to find other work. He

worried about the performance monitoring procedure in the warehouse:
It is permitted to work in the warehouse when you are higher efficiency 95% and more. I have only 95 and comma some.

Juliana and Ricardo felt a great deal of hostility and a total lack of respect from their superiors in the pizza factory:
In the factory, the manager, the team leaders .. they think we are .. animals. They treat us like animals.

Others were taken aback at the gulf between their prior expectations and the reality they encountered. Ona, unable to find a job at her level in Lithuania, arrived to the UK with a high level of expectation, since she had long harboured a high respect for the UK and was shocked to find that:
There was living twenty people in a house ... sleeping on the floors, you know, no beds, nothing .. they're getting the mattress from the streets ... It was young people ... coming here believing in this ... dream that you can earn lots of money and everything

Relationships with co-workers
For some, it was not easy to get along with co-workers due to perceived class or cultural differences.
you're just different and er the truth is that most people I've known er they were you know factory people ... so just like lower class so I don't know the lower class in Poland so I cannot compare .... they laugh at me because I read a book on the break .. they say "What is so interesting in a book? It's boring' .... So that made me feel that erm people are laughing at me cos I'm not maybe I'm not in my .. I'm not living in my correct class (Stanislaw).

Andrzej, as a qualified veterinary surgeon working in an animal laboratory, felt himself to be more expert about the animals in his care than his supervisors and had had altercations with them about their decisions which created a poor work atmosphere and eventually played a role in his dismissal:
English people is very hypocrite .. you tell er for example my team leader tell me .. "You are very good worker, superb" Two days later .. "Sorry" Out. Your job is very bad, out."

Edmund and Marjanna were shocked at what they perceived as a low work ethic among English workers, and found it annoying to break their own intense work rhythm because of the frequent breaks:
very strange for us in beginning here ... after two hours, yeah "Break

*Time!"... "Tea Time!" ... [laughs heartily] and two hours later,
"Lunchtime!" ... I mean .. how did you get the economical state of your
country if, if, if no one really works here? [laughs] I mean no one's .. no
one's doing anything.*

This sense of having a superior work ethic to the English and to other
ethnic minorities was widespread, especially among the Poles. The Polish, in
particular, seemed to be very aware of their reputation as hard workers, which
they felt was in stark contrast to the work ethic of minority groups. These
seemed to be singled out for harsh criticism and, at times, some quasi-racist
comments were expressed in interviews:

*We learn everything more quicker .... We just, .. doing properly, because
when we doing something we thinking. ... And that's why the English
people want to hire Polish people, not Indian people. The Indian people
they even, they have to really, really learn here everything. Because, I
know how in Indian is. In India it's really not good country and
everything, they are not I mean .. education. (Cecylja)*

*My workplace, Polish people are very good workers, yeah? That is why
many Polish people work in UK and just, when something is broke up,
Polish guy comes and [makes a swishing noise] it's working, yeah? And
in hospitals for example, there is a lot of, uh, Indian, er from India, yeah?
Why? [laughs] (Sebastian)*

Those interviewees who had, out of financial need, taken on jobs at a
lower level than jobs for which they were qualified, eventually began to notice
a change in their self-perception, which required them to reconcile their own
self-image. This often resulted in a feeling of frustration when they began to
sense that other people did not recognise their educational abilities.

Celine, who had passed her teacher training but failed her qualification
year, was working as a teaching assistant and felt frustrated that this led others
to undervalue her educational worth:

*Some people here think, think I've got no education. On a par with a
peanut, yes.*

This was all the more galling for her since, despite working at a lower
level than the teachers in her school, she knew in her heart that she was at
least as capable of teaching as they were:

*sometimes it's frustrating, because you go into lessons and I can see that
teachers, who are now having teaching careers, are not very good .. are
worse than I was.*

A similar sense of feeling ill at ease with oneself as a result of pressure from the looking glass self was evident in Marjanna's account, in which a sense of self doubt came through:

But if somebody .. tells you all the .... you know "You are not good enough" you starting to think about that like it's true, maybe I'm not good enough, yeah? Edmund always, always says "Just try believe in yourself. Just try to do something different and" ... but [sighs] ..... everybody thinks if I work in coffee shop, I'm just .. I'm not smart enough, ... because I can't find something better.

Coping techniques

Faced with monotonous job tasks, tiring and demanding work in a stressful environment, strained relations with co-workers and a conflict of selves, the migrants developed a number of coping techniques.

One technique adopted by those who decided to continue in their menial jobs was to strive to become noticed by their employer in order to be singled out for internal re-assignment or promotion because of a good attitude or because of specialised knowledge.

you need to try and show that you want to learn, that you want to do, it's not like they will come and offer just like that (Sofija).

they offered me to second his duties - part time, obviously, because I have other job - so I said "Well, why not?" So that's what I'm doing now (Edmund).

Andrzej, as a vet, was very successful when breeding rabbits in the laboratory, and his success did not go unnoticed:

I change every job. I change more procedure for er better job .. my er ... for example ... my mothers born 240 babies and maybe 3, maybe 5 babies is stillborn, is dead. Different people cycles born 210 and stillborn 40, 30 .. my team leader tell me 'How, how did you, what you make when your born is better, every, everything is better."... "'I can't talk you. I can write you." I write six page, every procedure which I make.

Paradoxically, Andrzej attributes his dismissal from the job to the threat he felt he posed to his supervisor:

when every people, every people which boss don't like .. broken by him and out er this method yes, my team leader and my supervisor is er maybe scared

This view was supported by Stanislaw:

If you are like blind and you do everything they .. want it's .. OK but if you er if you want to be more efficient, if you want to improve your job and you suggest something er many people didn't like it.

In these cases, the interviewees expressed frustration that their attempts to make themselves noticed by showing initiative seemed to backfire by irking those they reported to.

Another coping technique employed was evidenced by a willingness to invest in training in order to increase one's career capital. The importance of English language training has been referred to earlier. In addition to this, four of the interviewees, at times at their own expense, enrolled for a course of study or undertook vocational training courses which they felt would enhance their job prospects.

Stanislaw, whilst visiting his family in Poland over the Christmas period, paid for a training course as a forklift driver. He was motivated to do so as he knew that there was opportunity in the factory in which he worked for more lucrative work driving forklifts than in his current job:

erm I made my forklift licence in Poland, so you know, I paid for that ... between, er between Christmas and New Year's day er 2006 at Christmas ..... sometimes you have to, you know, sacrifice.

Gabriela, who showed a great thirst for knowledge, having enrolled on both English and Arabic classes, was also keen to build on the experience she had had working as an intern for the UN in Brazil:

I already got a place in the University to post graduate in International Security, to starting next September.

Sofija, like Stanislaw, was willing to invest her own money in her education by funding a course. Having been promoted into an administrative position, she was looking into the possibility of self funding a management course in order to try to apply for a position as an account manager in the same company:

The thing is, not usually you get like [funding] that from company, you need to find a company who will be, who would like to do that, but it's more easier if you do it on your own and then you can get a better job.

Brigita was enrolled on a conversion course for medical professionals wanting to work in the NHS. In addition, she had taken on unpaid voluntary work to enhance her CV and help her to find a suitable job.

A third coping technique was self-employment. Although only one of the interviewees (Pawel) successfully set himself up in business, Celine worked on a self-employed basis for a publisher and on a contract basis as an interpreter. Edmund and his wife Marjanna mentioned the idea of setting up a business together, explaining that a restaurant serving Polish dishes or a delicatessen offering imported Polish food would be a viable business proposition. For all except Pawel, however, the sacrifices and demands such a choice entailed were currently not an option, given the desire for steady employment and the difficulty of obtaining credit. However, the possibility of setting up a business should they decide to remain in the UK was in the back of their minds.

we were thinking of starting some kind of a business here we just need money for that and to have money you either take a loan or something but then again being a Polish doesn't make me easier to get a loan for that (Edmund).

Pawel, however, having seen his first business succeed beyond his expectations, was already starting a second one. He had been surprised to discover his entrepreneurial streak and had succeeded in the area of painting and decorating, one in which he had no prior experience:

it's now five people employed in full time and four people self employed who we work with and it probably will expand into about two, three more, which will be about twelve people this year.

After this initial positive experience, he began to think of other business possibilities, and was co-investing in:

.. a relocation company, like people who like to relocate to Poland, preferably it would be both ways... And it's more and more people, actually emigrating to Poland, so.. what we've done with this other business, we've got a website at the moment and we started doing some networking and meeting and things like that ..

Pawel had taught English prior to coming to the UK and, at the time of interviewing, had been here for two and a half years. These factors seemed to give him the confidence to become an entrepreneur. The fact that he was also in a permanent relationship with an Englishman perhaps also helped him to gain the confidence and know-how needed for such a step.

Changing jobs

The interviewees were often forced through lack of funds to take on a temporary job. Once they had managed to obtain some form of temporary employment and earn enough to survive, however, they set their sights on procuring permanent employment. The desire to find permanent or at least longer term work was mentioned by eight of the interviewees.

Their job search strategies, though perhaps not explicitly acknowledged during the interviews, seemed to prioritise certain factors.

Although an awareness of their lack of career capital (especially English language skills) helped to prevent them from seeking more suitable work, it also served to give them the courage to seek other jobs. Thus, Ona wasted no time in cashing in on her relatively advanced English language skills in order to escape from the disappointment she felt after taking up the job in the Lincolnshire onion fields which she had procured in Lithuania:

> *In the onion fields, for a box, you can get five pounds so ... in a day ... let's say four boxes ... twenty pounds ... plus they're taking the money from the travelling, from the house and everything like that. So when I went there I said 'No way. I'm not going to do that.'.. I didn't stay in that agency cos I said "Listen I know .. English. I'm going to go to the job centre. I'm going to look for a job somewhere else. I'll find it. It doesn't matter where.*

However, Valeska was frustrated at the range of jobs available to her.
> *the same day I found in, I work a job in warehouse. It was like from rain to under gutter, [=out of the frying pan, into the fire] yeah? From [care] home to warehouse, it was a similar job.*

Such frustration may persuade migrants to return to their home country, should they feel that there is no further escape possible.

The desire for permanent work was not the same as the desire for work commensurate with their qualifications and abilities. The former was seen as necessary for financial survival, whereas the latter was a more distant aspiration, and one for which it was not uncommon to feel unready. An awareness of their lack of career capital (especially English language skills) served to hold them back from seeking more suitable work and a reluctance was shown to risk losing what they already had.

Jiri, the eldest interviewee at 56, had been in the same job since arriving two years previously and was very concerned about losing it. Although he found the work very demanding physically, he was not interested in alternatives:

> *I am quite afraid about the tax because in the new work you must work for several months before receiving contract and it's going worse and worse now this situation yes for the foreign nations here, mostly for the Polish because the Polish are the most frequent nationality. So, I do not think about the change, I will be in this work till I will not be dispelled.*

Marjanna, who was becoming increasingly frustrated at the inability to use her new degree in Accounting, was torn between leaving the coffee shop she worked in and the relative security it offered:

I'm really tired when I come back home and Edmund always says OK, Marjanna, you need to find something different because you drive me crazy with that job. Just try to, to find something better. Just do it for yourself."And it was good excuse for me" But Edmund, you know, it's permanent work, if I find something worse it will be .. worse for us, yeah?"

Sofija, who was promoted out of the blue, felt an initial pang of panic on the appointment:

They just push me into it, actually. He was, like, we change the shift, yeah and I came back from my day off and they just said That's it, you're not working here anymore, you're going now to the office. I said, er, "I don't know anything about it, what it is, why, what's going on?" Like it was quite shock for me and they said "Yeah, we can see that you can do it and just, and person is leaving in two days so you just need to take over." I said "OK", and I thought Oh God, I don't want to go, I like my job where I am. I'm not important, but I do like it."

Cecylja, who had been able to find some temporary work more suited to her administrative background, decided instead to accept an offer of a permanent post in a canteen, arguing that the permanent nature of the job was more important than the nature of the work itself:

.. my friend just called me and I can doing a job in a canteen, just work for that company. And then she said this is a job from they say permanent job. You've got everything, holiday, everything. And that was for me what was important, have a permanent job. Because, in Poland I've got a mortgage for my flat and I have to pay that and then, ... for that I've got a job, every day and not just you know, waiting for a call from the agency "Oh you cannot go to work today" or "May be you can go". That was for me very important and that's why I just agreed to that.

For Edmund, who was successful in finding a job which utilized some of his IT skills, the sense of security it offered by dint of being permanent was a major attraction and enabled him to keep his options open:

I just came over here .. found job. "Yeah, why not? I might stay here". Now when I do have a permanent job I'm thinking of staying for some time just because this country suits me now.

Sebastian had a definite plan to leave after six months or so, once he had saved enough to join his girlfriend in Amsterdam, and begin his Master's degree in Musicology there. However, he was very aware of the possibility of staying longer should he so wish:

It's an open [contract]. I can stay here, I think, many years [laughs] ... There's a lot of people who are working in this factory. For example, Kenya is fifteen years.

Sofija was not happy to remain in temporary part time posts and was very proactive in finding a permanent post:

I started in one agency, but it wasn't quite good, I had job maybe two or three times a week, it wasn't enough and then I just find agency .. where I went to, made my application form and I had the job and, you know, ... I get the permanent work, the proper work, from agency .. it was .. every day, which was good.

Veronika, whose post with the Council at the time of the interview required her to monitor migrant workers and try to find solutions to their problems, also highlighted the lack of full time work as an issue of concern:

er, the main problem is, you know, to get as much work as possible ... what is happening now is agencies are taking too many people and they're not supplying them, with, you know, like even forty hours a week. You know, some of them working only four days and you know, when you don't earn as much, then so obviously it's concern.

The skill- and status- underemployment that they experienced in their jobs meant that the migrants had to cope with the demands of the physical nature of the work; the repetitive nature of the work; the stressful working environment; relationships with co-workers; and their own social perceptions in the eyes of others. They adopted several techniques to try and cope with these demands. These included trying very hard to make a good impression on their employers; undergoing training, especially English language training; setting up in business, and an ongoing search for more secure jobs, if possible ones which were more commensurate with their qualifications and experience.

Chapter 7: Impact of nonwork and family factors on adjustment to living and working in the UK

A sense of surprise was evident when the migrants compared their prior expectations of the UK with the reality they encountered. This was most marked for those migrants who had not previously visited the UK.

I always wanted to go to the UK. I don't know why. It was a kind of dream [laughs].....It's completely opposite, it's so completely opposite of my .. imagination .. basically ... from outside UK looks so .. great, so .. different but when you come here, I'm sorry, to say that, ... the environment and the people over here ..when I came here I said 'Gosh, where I am? It's really UK? It's really England?" (Ona)

I imagined that you had very high culture, because you were leaders, powerful. Yeah and inventions. You .. Western society was more civilised, more culture... but .. It is like American lifestyle is like a drug, epidemic, ... and people behave like, like majority in any society, in any group, like in television, they saw, yeah. (Valeska)

Among the cultural differences the main one noted was a predilection for alcohol abuse by the English, which was negatively viewed by the interviewees:

what I've noticed ... people like to work themselves out for a week and then piss themselves out on the weekend and that's not my way of spending free time I'm just not fancying alcohol in very large quantities Looking at the .. looking at the behaviour of the British people you are drunks (Edmund).

Every day I'm seeing people here drunk. They fight, they fight on public transport. I never seen a drunk man in a house before in Holland. I witness it here. (Kamal)

and.. addictiveness for alcohol or socialising with alcohol with bad way. (Valeska)

81

Such observations which stir up a general sense of distaste and even of revulsion, are important insofar as they restrict the migrants' potential for socialisation. Repelled by their English acquaintances, they were less likely to mix with them and this had an affect on their progress in English as well as their general feelings towards the UK. Their relationships with their fellow countrymen were also not always amicable. Consequently, they could be said to be living on the margins of both the local community and their own community.

Another noticeable reaction was one of incredulity towards the multicultural nature of 21st century UK society. Migrants who had not given any thought to the location of their jobs and who had little or no experience or knowledge of the UK, were surprised to see a high proportion of ethnic minority groups and struggled to accept their presence. This further marginalised the migrant community.

> *you can't see white people over more than different .. I mean, ethnic groups and everything ... it was bit surprising for me because I expected more white people over here [laughs] (Ona).*

> *Now I know, here it's the biggest population of Indian people here in England. But, it surprised me, really. (Cecylja)*

Absence of the family

The importance placed on extended family as "significant others" was evident in this study. This finding emphasises the importance of the family from an individual perspective both before and during migration.

The lived experiences of the interviewees outside of work was clearly influenced by their family status. Six of the seven single interviewees and eleven of the twelve married ones had extended family back home. The two exceptions were Veronika, who had been joined by her parents and her brother in the house she had bought in the East of England, and Gabriela, whose parents came out from Brazil to help her with her three small children. In these cases, the extended family members returned to the home country when necessary, and there was an open invitation for other members of the extended family to stay if they wanted to seek work or spend a holiday in the UK.

> *[My father] I don't know if he will stay, he's planning to go in July again back, for Brazil to come back. My mother is coming to stay with me, definitely. But he's .. maybe he will come to stay like some part, some months he stay there, some months he stay with me. My sister is there also. I say to he, I want your life. You stay some months there, some months here, very good life." He's agree. I have one brother also, he's coming*

tomorrow .. to find work. (Gabriela)

Veronika and Gabriela both expressed concern that their parents were finding it very hard to learn English. Veronika's parents had struggled to keep their farm in Latvia going but had found employment locally despite their lack of ability in English:

Er actually, my Mum and Dad and my brother is here now .... they're very happy here. Erm, Mum and Dad, they don't speak English very well. Mum is trying to improve her English. With my Dad it's much harder, because he's, erm, he's learned German before so that's why he's problems now. He picks up bits. I've taught him how to count, how to - the basic words, what he needs in the packhouse - they work in the packhouse like packhouse operative (Veronika).

Gabriela tried to make her parents feel more at home by installing Brazilian cable TV:

for them, what they .. what I .. noticed, the language is a problem. Because they .. but then I put the cable TV, they watch the Brazilian programmes (Gabriela).

For the vast majority of the interviewees, however, the extended family were left behind. However, the relative low cost and rapid speed of travel to the home country, together with the freedom of movement they enjoyed, enabled the migrants to visit home easily. This assuaged any guilt they felt about missing family events such as weddings, and funerals and allowed them to visit sick relatives if necessary.

I've been just recently visiting grandma. She's not very well. And I went to my cousin's wedding. (Veronika)

last year, for wedding my godson .. but ... four days only. ... I went .. to see my grandparents, because my grandparents very old people and I see them. (Isabella)

Similarly, the two interviewees whose spouses had remained in the home country were able to visit, or be visited by, them frequently. The role of modern communication technologies also helped to keep them in touch. For those interviewees whose spouse was living in the home country, technology played a large part in reducing the isolation they felt:

We have constant communication, so it's not big sacrifice or something. Like was in past, the past that you should send letters and they go .. ten days. It's like we can communicate every day. (Valeska)

Other migrants

The six single interviewees in the study and the two married interviewees with spouses left behind found it financially necessary to share accommodation with others. Sebastian and Stanislaw were lifelong friends and had no problems sharing. Valeska shared with other migrants to save money, but had minimal contact with them:

> *I live in accommodation house with different people, but in separate room and I don't speak to them. The Polish are my closest neighbours. ... They are sitting, drinking, smoking, talking all the time and .. behave like pigs.*

Such isolation from the wider English speaking community outside of work had a clear effect on the development of the interviewees' command of English, as put succinctly by Andrzej:

> *I live four months only myself, no Polish people, I working four months no Polish people. This progress [in the English language] is very very quickly, for me. After this four months, I live again with Polish people. My progress is kaputt.*

Conversely, Sofija, who had been staying with her boyfriend and his aunt, broke away soon after arrival and sought out others who spoke neither English nor Latvian:

> *I changed the house that was quite different, they were mixed .. Portuguese, South African. The main language that you can contact with them is English, so whichever people can speak what kind of English they can, that way we were talking.*

Interaction with co-workers outside of work was minimal. As a result, the interviewees socialised either only with those of a similar educational and national background to themselves, or with extended family already in the UK and their acquaintances.

Edmund and his wife Marjanna, who both had family members living within a few miles, found the behaviour of many of their fellow countrymen repugnant and so tended to move in very small social circles:

> *I find that er spending time with Polish people in this country is not suiting my level of er behaviour. A lot of them are behaving worse than they would do in Poland. The only people from Poland we just meet is closest friends we know here. We don't really meet new Polish people in this country.*

This lack of empathy was shared by Cecylja, whose negative views on her compatriots echoed her stereotypical portrayal of ethic minorities. She also restricted her social circle:

most people from Poland who came here they are not educated and not want to learn even here English, or doing something higher and they are just, er, they are simply, really simply ..... But, 10 % people want to do something more. Learn, you know, get more skills, qualifications, doing something more. And then come back to Poland with something .. The most people, they want to stay here and do nothing, because here it's really easy. Easier than in Poland, because, you earn money here, you just spend for a beer, it's like you know, that level ..... So, I'm not really happy with the Polish people here. I just got some friends, really really, few friends and that's it.

Jiri, at 56, was unlikely to bond with the ex-flatmates of his 20-year-old daughter, with whom he stayed after his daughter had returned home to study. Their lifestyle choices were clearly at odds with his own:

They are till now here but they are the kind of people which I must say I do not like very much .. I think that men .. must have some purpose in life and I do not like this phrase "I came to England to live and I do not want to work. I do not know what I will be doing next year. I do not know how long I will be here."... I do not like er this kind of Polish people ... which are spending all the money for smoking, er, buying the food, er for buying the drug, for drugs, yes, so they are these kind, these two acquaintance with my daughter so I'm not living now with them.

Sebastian, who shared a house with Stanislaw, was comfortable with other educated Poles but started to avoid Polish people he did not know, as he found them rather preoccupied with work matters:

many Polish people when we meet, for example, someone in supermarket, yeah? The first question: "Where, where are you working? How much you get paid for, for, for the hour?" or something this. It's a stupid question, yeah? It's the first, not like "How are you?" "What are you doing?"for example, oh.. normal conversation. But no. "How much?" "Where?" OK. [laughs] And just, wow. "Sorry, I just want to buy something."

Polish communities were well established in all the venues in which the interviews with the Polish interviewees took place. However, the Polish interviewees were not interested in mixing with the Polish community who had emigrated just after the Second World War, and neither did they frequent the Polish churches.

The existence of community associations for the non-Polish interviewees varied depending upon nationality and venue. Only Brigita made reference to her national association, which she took advantage of to help her children gain experience of performing in concerts:

'There is a Lithuanian Community who needs er some young people, performing people, as my children. My daughter is violin player and er she can play piano as well and my son he came here he plays accordion and piano and they say they need these people, so we went and we had Easter Concert, you know, with the UK band and it was lovely. Everybody was happy [laughs].

The migrants were faced with the need to adjust to both work and nonwork situations. Their adjustment was affected by nonwork and family factors, with beneficial effects on significant others, particularly children, offsetting negative aspects of the job to a degree. Their migration had an impact on both their nuclear and extended family both here and in the home country. Their nonwork adjustment was also affected by marginalisation from UK society but also from other migrants, whom they considered to be of a lower social class than themselves. This was especially the case with the Polish migrants.

Having examined the experiences of the interviewees in each of these four areas, it is to a discussion of how these factors combine that we now turn. This discussion will provide us with a clearer understanding of the experiences of such migrants during their time in the UK, and so provide new insights into new forms of international working.

Conclusions

Mixed Motivations

In the analysis of the motivations which lay behind the migrants' decision to leave their home countries and to come to the UK to work, a number of push and pull factors were identified. As was to be expected from previous studies of similar migrants (Cook, Dwyer & Waite, 2011; Trevena, 2006; Drinkwater, Eade & Garapich, 2006; Currie, 2006; Spencer et al, 2007), the most visible of these were financial incentives. The widespread mention of finances as a motivating factor (by fourteen of the nineteen interviewees) reflected a number of reasons. These included an urgent need for money due to debts or family pressure; a desire to accumulate funds to sponsor ongoing or future studies or investments; a desire to earn enough to be comfortable without having to work long hours; and a desire simply to be able to work at all and earn a living. Money, then, was both a push factor, insofar as lack of money served as a driver to look for work overseas, and a pull factor insofar as the prospect of being able to command a higher financial reward in the UK loomed high as a motivator.

However, there was clear evidence from the interviews that financial considerations do not necessarily dominate the decision to come to the UK. This resonates with the claim that financial incentives are only one force among many in a much more complicated picture of motivations of A8 migrants in the UK than is frequently assumed in the popular psyche (Cook, Dwyer & Waite, 2011; Bell, Jarman & Lefebvre, 2004; Schneider & Holman, 2009; McKay & Winkelmann-Gleed, 2005 ;Trevena, 2009). Apart from the fact that five of the nineteen interviewees did not refer to money at all when explaining their motives in coming to the UK, six of those who mentioned financial incentives as playing a role in their decision to come to the UK also mentioned non-economic factors such as a desire to explore a new culture or to learn English. The possibility of improving one's education, or of providing an opportunity for one's children to get a better education was mentioned by six interviewees as a key factor in their decision to come here, with financial incentives a minor factor.

The importance of non-economic considerations instead of, or alongside, financial ones in the analysis of the motivations of a group of individuals often referred to as "economic migrants" should not be overlooked. Should government bodies or employers in the UK wish to attract more migrant workers to fill positions here, they may be well advised to do so by giving some consideration as to how non-economic factors can be enhanced, rather than concentrating solely on economic factors. During the recession which started in 2008, the fall in the value of sterling against many Eastern European currencies prompted reports of a mass exodus of A8 migrant workers. It is beyond the scope of this study to examine the veracity of such claims. However, this study makes a tentative suggestion that a proportion of the migrants might be less affected by such economic obstacles as fluctuating currency rates if other strong pull factors, such as the availability and cost of educational opportunities, were made more affordable and attainable.

The decision to come may also have been affected by a sense of not wanting to miss out on an 'adventure'. This was true of four of the nineteen interviewees - Schneider & Holman (2009) found that a similar proportion of their interviewees expressed the notion of 'adventure' as a motivating force. Even among those interviewees who did not explicitly mention adventure as a motivation, the freedom of movement within the EU which they enjoyed played a significant role in their decision to come to the UK on an open-ended and non-binding basis. Since they did not need to decide in advance how long they would stay, the interviewees could dip a toe in the water. Edmund decided to stay with his sister and "see what happens"; Pawel and Sofija both accompanied friends here who were keener than they were to settle (and who ironically left quickly); Jiri objected to this attitude of "I came to England to live and I do not want to work. I do not know what I will be doing next year. I do not know how long will I be here." among his younger compatriots. This ability to come to the UK 'on spec' with the ability to return home easily and cheaply underlies Favell's (2008) claim that migrants from A8 countries should not be studied using the mindset of more traditional immigration studies, since they are actually 'free movers', who frequently return home for short trips (Drinkwater, Eade & Garapich, 2006).

The importance of the freedom of movement which the interviewees enjoyed is also reflected by the decision of thirteen of the interviewees to come to the UK without having first arranged a job. The six interviewees who had arranged a job prior to departure were to change jobs soon after arrival, in one case immediately. Felker (2011) found that the educated A8 migrants in her study typically did not research the job market before departure. The present study supports that finding and notes that migrants did not pay much attention to the geographical location within the UK in which they were placed by agencies in their home countries. Those interviewees who were placed in UK jobs by home country agencies gave little or no consideration to the location of their work here, failing to take into consideration regional differences in the UK in terms of labour market composition, unemployment rates or relative costs of living. Similarly, they showed a lack of awareness of the proportion of ethnic minorities within the workforce.

The ad hoc nature of the geographical placement of the migrant workers in the UK reinforces Felker's (2011) claim that employers in regions with specific skill shortages are missing out on potentially valuable employees. The arbitrary choice of destination which the migrants make does little to alleviate the possibility that they will end up in a situation of skill- and status-underemployment.

The migrants' decision to take up or seek work in the UK was also brought about as a result of push factors. The findings support the claim by Kazlauskiene and Rinkevcius (2006) that the decision to migrate was most prevalent among those who had been unable to find employment and those who were only in temporary employment. Five of the interviewees stated that their inability to find any work at all in their home country played a major role in persuading them to seek work in the UK. The same number cited dissatisfaction with the job which they had been doing prior to departure for the UK as a factor in persuading them to leave their home country. Although the impermanent nature of the home country job did exert an influence, there was also some support for the role of skill- and status- underemployment in the home country job as exerting a push factor. Although the small sample precludes pursuing this line of enquiry, it would be of potential interest to ascertain to what extent being overeducated for a home country job makes potential migrants more likely to settle for a job in the UK which does not utilise their qualifications and experience.

In four cases, the sense of disillusionment was not restricted to aspects of the work environment but extended to the nonwork environment also, such as a feeling that life in the home country outside of work had very little of interest to offer. The majority of research into expatriate adjustment seems to be centred on work factors (Grinstein & Wathieu, 2008; Andreason, 2008). This finding suggests an interesting additional source of enquiry into not only how individuals adjust to nonwork factors in a new country but how such factors persuade them to initiate a move in the first place.

Although the separation of motivating factors into "push" and "pull" factors is a longstanding and useful distinction, it is not always straightforward to separate pull and push factors as these are often intricately interwoven. For Andrzej and Stanislaw, for example, the 'pull' of 'good money' in UK jobs was an antidote to the 'push' of a pressing need for finances. Andrzej was in serious debt and had left Poland under a cloud, while Stanislaw was eager to get together a large sum of money as quickly as he could in order to fund his mother's cancer operation. For Brigita, the desire to give her children a better education was driven by the pull factor of world class education such as that her daughter later enjoyed at the Birmingham Conservatoire. However, it was also sparked by the lack of such opportunities for her children in Lithuania. Gabriela explained how the religious harassment she had suffered in Brazil after converting to Islam pushed her towards emigrating and also how the possibility of learning Arabic and helping her children to learn Islamic teachings had exerted a strong 'pull'. Thus, despite the convenience of the push and pull framework (Lee, 1966), it would appear to be difficult to separate the two sets of driving forces in real life examples.

Another factor which played a role in persuading migrants to come to the UK was the existence of family and friends already in the UK. Boneva & Frieze (2001) argue that such a network is not enough to trigger the decision to migrate. However, this study's findings show that its influence should not be underestimated. There are several examples of interviewees being persuaded to come to the UK by friends and family already here. Edmund explained how his sister had bought him a ticket to the UK and so made up his mind for him. Jiri explained how he had had his accommodation arranged by his daughter who had just returned to her home country. Juliana and Ricardo "caught the next plane" after hanging up the phone on friends in the UK, who persuaded them to leave their gruelling jobs in Germany to seek work there. Kamal sacrificed a high flying job with Médecins Sans Frontières in Den Haag at the insistence of his wife who simply wanted to be near to her family members in the UK. Sebastian's decision to come to the UK to raise money for his future Master's study in Holland crystallised after his lifelong friend Stanislaw invited him over. Sofija was reluctant to come at first until offered accommodation by her boyfriend's aunt in the East of England. In all these cases, the support, even cajolement, of friends and relatives in the UK seemed to bring about a tipping point in the decision to move here.

As McKay & Winkelmann-Gleed, 2005 point out, a decision such as that of leaving one country to seek work in another is the culmination of a complex mixture of many factors. For example, Valeska was motivated by a desire to leave Poland and to escape a life of unemployment ('push'); a plan to earn money ('pull'); a wish to learn English ('pull') and the pursuit of adventure ('pull'). Edmund was attracted by the possibility of earning money ('pull')' and a dislike of the long hours and travel involved in his previous job ('push'). Yet his decision to move only came about as a result of his sister's intervention in sending him a ticket to stay with her.

Such real world complex cases suggest that the ease and simplicity of the push and pull framework in analyses of migrants' motivations to come to the UK need to be balanced against the "…complexity and multi-levelled nature of explanations for international migration" (Robinson & Carey, 2000:89).

Yet, such a move is not one that every potential migrant will make. Lee (1966) stresses the force exerted by previous experience of migration in persuading people to commit to a move. This is reinforced by Drinkwater's (2003) findings that the willingness to move of individuals who have spent any time living abroad is significantly higher than those who have not previously lived outside of their home country Around a third of the interviewees mentioned previous visits to the UK, with a further three mentioning having spent time in other overseas countries. Thus, almost half of the respondents attributed time spent outside of their home countries with the decision to come to the UK. What is important in such cases is the migrant's perceptions of familiarity with the UK. In reality, the UK they had visited may be far removed from the UK in which they now find themselves. For example, Celine cited her familiarity with the UK as a result of an exchange with a pen friend "in year nine". Clearly, much had changed in the intervening 20 years or so. Yet her warm memories of that time made her more amenable to the idea of coming here to work.

Again, the influence of the freedom of movement enjoyed by EU citizens cannot be underestimated. There is clearly a need to take the conditions and determining factors that affect people's choices and opportunities to move into account (Ferro, 2006). Carling's (2002) model focussed on the reasons why those who wished to migrate may *not* be able to do so due to a combination of macro factors (the socially constructed meaning of migration and the emigration environment, consisting of the historical, social, economic, cultural or political setting which encourages or discourages migration) and micro level factors, (such as gender, age, family migration history, social status, educational attainment and personality traits). There is scope for a model such as Carling's to be devised which examines the factors enabling, rather than restraining, people's decisions to move. This might address the role and influence of macro factors such as EU membership and the 'eurostars' mindset (Favell, 2008) and micro factors such as prior visits to the UK, in encouraging a move.

Typologies of motivations

Several studies of A8 migrants (Trevena, 2006; 2010; Drinkwater, Eade & Garapich, 2006) made an attempt to create a typology based on their strategy and intentions. This study contends that, given the frequent changes in planned length of stay which migrants undergo after arrival (McKay & Winkelmann-Gleed, 2005), such plans may evolve not before but after arrival. This implies that we should be cautious about ascribing premeditated strategies to the migrants' actions.

For a minority of the interviewees, those with a clear strategy and intended period of stay, such strict categories would initially appear to be a helpful way of categorising them. Juliana and Ricardo set out to pay off a mortgage in three years then return home. Sebastian gave himself a time limit in which to save enough to do a Master's in Amsterdam. All three were adamant that they would leave the UK shortly. However, the snapshot nature of this study leaves open the possibility that they may decide to stay on, perhaps having found a job which is more lucrative, enjoyable or challenging. This is a drawback of a non-longitudinal approach.

The importance of time to an understanding of the migrants' career experiences is crucial. Sullivan (1999:474) pointed out that "The meaning of one job at one point in time lacks context." For many of the interviewees, it is hard to identify the context of the work they were doing at the time of the interview. For them it might represent a temporary stopgap job whilst they seek more desirable work, a job they are happy to stay in for the long term or a horrible but necessary means of survival from which they decide to escape by leaving the UK. Without a longitudinal approach, it is impossible for us to ascertain what route they will follow. The temptation to group individuals together based on a temporary stage in their career search should be resisted if we are to accept that they may end up following very different paths.

Overeducated employees have been found to be more likely to seek a job change (Robst, 1995; Sicherman, 1991). The interviewees' accounts of when and why they changed jobs seem to suggest that the situation in which they found themselves at the time of the interview was more the result of an ongoing development process than that of a premeditated plan. The freedom of movement which EU citizens enjoy enables them to stay on as their initial intentions change. This ability to vary one's intended length of stay, to experiment whilst here in a variety of jobs and nonwork situations, empowers migrant workers to develop new and unexpected goals and plans whilst here, which may differ greatly from their original intentions before departure.

Pawel, for example, initially came over to accompany a friend who left soon afterwards, intending to return after the summer break. His main motivation in coming and staying on after the summer was that it was a bit of an 'adventure'. His decision to set himself up as self-employed in a field (painting and decorating) of which he had no prior experience, came as a shock even to himself and did not reflect a prior intention before departure. His nonwork situation also changed when he found a life partner, which also changed his intended length of stay.

Similarly, Edmund explained how he had arrived at his sister's insistence claiming that "I've never had that [looking for work in the UK] on my mind. I just came over here .. found job. "Yeah why not? I might stay here". Once he had found a permanent job which utilised some of his skills and experience, however, he stated that "I'm thinking of staying for some time just because this country suits me now." It is hard to envisage how this shift in focus and strategy which Edmund undergoes would fit into preconceived categories within a typology. To allow for an understanding of how his attitudes and goals changed during his time here would necessitate allowing for the possibility that he set out as one type of migrant and then became another.

He, and many others like him, are primarily affected not by a pre-existing set of characteristics which identify them as a member of a group, but by the nature of the jobs that they obtain. Given the effects of skill- and status-underemployment on migrants' identities, any such typology would need to enable us to know how failure to find a permanent, fulfilling job would have affected Edmund's outlook. It seems likely that he would be classified as belonging to a different category in a migrant typology if he had been interviewed just before he found his present job.

Therefore, this study echoes critique of typologies as consisting of ideal categories into which actual migrants may not necessarily fit. Over time, the complexity of the ongoing motivational forces being experienced by migrants, and especially the change in outlook they experience when finding work which they regard as more suitable, render such typologies too rigid. Rather than fit migrants into neat categories, this study argues that each individual's outlook will be affected by their experiences. As Louis (1980) points out, the way in which individuals react to such changes in their lives will vary. Such experiences, especially that of finding a job which appeals, may persuade those who planned to stay long term but who grew disillusioned to leave early or those who arrived with a sceptical mindset to stay on for longer. There is clearly a need for more longitudinal studies to illuminate such cases.

Barriers

The second research question asked what barriers the migrants faced in finding work commensurate with their skills and qualifications. The main reasons identified were a lack of English language skills, a reluctance on the part of agencies and potential employers to recognise non-UK qualifications and experience, and a lack of funds sufficient to finance a long job search.

An inability to function linguistically at a professional level has been seen to create a barrier to employment of otherwise suitably qualified and experienced candidates (Lianos, 2007; Patrinos, 1997; Nielsen, 2007: Liversage, 2009; Bauder, 2003; Kler, 2006; Green, Kler and Leeves, 2007; Waddington, 2007; Battu & Sloane, 2002; OECD, 2006). This problem has also been identified among migrants in the UK (Trevena, 2006; Currie, 2006:

bSolutions 2005) especially among older migrants (Battu and Sloane, 2002; Dustmann and Fabbri, 2003). It is beyond the scope of this study to ascertain whether the level of English on arrival affected the migrants' ability to obtain more challenging jobs, since to determine that would require a longitudinal approach. What is clear, however, is that those interviewees who were successful in obtaining more challenging jobs stressed the need for good English, whether this was obtained prior to arrival (e.g. Celine, Pawel) or subsequently (e.g. Sofija, Veronika), as an important aspect of their success.

Others' failure to improve their command of the language significantly was not always the result of a lack of motivation. As shown by Spencer et al. (2005) the migrants with the greatest need to improve their English tend to take on menial jobs with shift patterns which make it very difficult for them to attend classes. This creates a vicious circle in which their English fails to improve, meaning that they are unable to enhance their language ability sufficiently in order to obtain any other employment. Jiri, Sebastian and Valeska all expressed difficulties in attending classes because of their work schedules. Cecylja saw one of the main benefits of her permanent canteen job as being able to attend English classes regularly. Those interviewees who lacked confidence in their English ability were happy to take on menial work if this gave them the opportunity to attend English classes. Both Sofija and Veronika put a great deal of effort into learning the language and ascribed this as a key reason for their success in obtaining a promotion and a council job respectively.

The interviewees also took steps to improve their command of English outside of the classroom. Educated migrants are frequently unable to spend any time with educated native speakers (Spencer et al., 2007) and may shun the company of less educated locals and workmates (Trevena, 2009). For example, Stanislaw felt uneasy alongside his "lower class [colleagues, who] laugh at me because I read a book on the break ... may be ... I'm not living in my correct class". Edmund, Kamal and Brigita all expressed repulsion at locals' binge drinking and spent little time with native speakers.

Some individuals mentioned that distancing themselves from their fellow countrymen was an effective aid in learning English. Andrzej reported how he had progressed rapidly in his command of the language in the four months which he had spent living apart from his compatriots and that this progress had been stemmed when he moved in with his fellow Poles again. Sofija was determined to improve her shaky English and so moved in with non-native speakers with different mother tongues to her, forcing English to be used as a lingua franca between them.

Professional associations and hiring bodies may find fault with immigrants' credentials and create barriers preventing them from entering their chosen profession (Bauder, 2003; Currie, 2006). Pemberton (2008) found that employment agencies in the North West of England pushed migrants into accepting initial 'foot in the door' unskilled work offers which did not take account of their skills. This was certainly evident in the accounts given by some of the interviewees. Marjanna and Edmund expressed frustration at the dismissive treatment they received in employment agencies and Pawel found it impossible to convince employers and agencies of the value of his Polish teaching credentials.

The migrants' ability to find jobs at their educational level was also hindered by their lack of funds. Those who arrived without a job arranged soon found their financial resources dwindling. Andrzej, for example, explained how he soon finished all the money he had brought with him - £300 - in London and so had no choice other than to take any job he could get. Kamal eventually became resigned to the fact that he would have to compromise on the nature of the job he took on if he were to be able to survive financially in the short term. Such cases reflected previous findings that workers may temporarily accept jobs for which they are overqualified because of the costs involved in finding a more appropriate job (Johnson, 1978; Jovanovic, 1979). The danger here is that if the temporary job gradually becomes a long-term job, the negative effects of overeducation are more likely to be felt. There is some indication that, once employed, the migrants found it difficult to search for other jobs, often due to the antisocial hours they were working. To gain a fuller picture of how overeducation becomes a permanent rather than a temporary phenomenon in the lives of educated migrants such as those in this study is again something which can only be ascertained by a longitudinal study.

Coping

The third research question asked how the migrants coped with the skill- and status- underemployment in the jobs they took on. The adjustments which the migrants had to come to terms with were: the physical nature of the work; the repetitive nature of the work; the stressful working environment; relationships with co-workers; and their own social perceptions in the eyes of others.

Louis' (1980) typology of transitions identified three common features – change, contrast and surprise. Changes were defined as objective, clear and often predictable differences, whereas contrasts were explained as the subjective experience by the transitioner of the changes, thus an internal perspective as opposed to the external perspective of changes. By surprises were meant the differences between an individual's anticipations of future experiences and the actual events. Surprises are positive or negative subjective appreciations of the differences between one's expectations of a new role and one's subsequent actual experiences.

This emphasis on the subjective experiences of transitioners is important to an understanding of the migrants' lived experiences during their Interprofession Transitions (Louis, 1980) in which they changed from one profession to another, and were placed in in a different, or 'foreign' culture with a different terminology, altered interpersonal and professional interactions, and an unfamiliar sense of professional identity.

In contrast to most studies citing Louis's (1980) model, however, (Black, Gregersen & Mendenhall 1992; Harvey 1997; Hippler 2000; Blau, 2000; Thompson & van de Ven, 2002; Ebaugh, 1988; Kulkarni, Lengnick-Hall & Valk, 2010; Bruce and Scott, 1994) the present study seeks to understand how the migrants adapt to *downward* transitions, an aspect which has not received much attention in the careers literature (Newman, 1999; Slay, 2006; Rooth & Ekberg, 2006; Remennick, 1999; Miller, Haskell, & Thatcher, 2002).

Such transitions often result in a decrease in self esteem (Trevena, 2010; Zikic et al, 2010) which is exacerbated by real or imagined perceptions of our looking glass selves (Cooley, 1902) and by the effect of a low social status within society (Johnson, 2000). As migrants continue in their jobs, and begin to sense that there may not be a way out of such employment, they may develop a reduced self image as their looking glass self begins to assert itself over their own self image (Trevena, 2006). This is seen for example in Marjanna's self questioning of her ability to hold down a job other than that of a coffee shop waitress despite her accountancy degree, in Andrzej's gradual depression after losing his job working with animals and the last hopes of putting his veterinary degree to any use here and in Celine's frustration at not being allowed to teach when her colleagues were so ineffective in the classroom.

Nicholson's 1990 Transition Cycle Model (Nicholson, 1990) appeared at first to be a suitable tool for analysing the downward transitions experienced by the migrants, as it allowed for the potential of failure in transitions. However, Nicholson's model was not developed with non-organisational transitions in mind. It appears less applicable to cases in which the degree of change is not within predictable organisational boundaries. Further, it ignores many essential aspects of geographical relocation, such as family pressures and linguistic challenges. There is scope for an enhanced version of the model which would enhance the existing aspects by adding the ability to account for the extra layers of complexity encountered by migrant workers seeking or taking up work overseas which are brought about by the cultural changes they face and the downward transition they undergo with its effects on their sense of self esteem and identity.

There were three major reasons why it was felt that Louis' (1980) model was best suited to this study. Firstly, the simplicity of the model exerted a strong appeal. It encapsulated three very simple but compelling criteria for the study of any transition: change, contrast, and surprise. This toolkit seemed to offer the researcher more flexibility than other models examined. Secondly, Louis' model has been seen as relevant in a large number of studies of expatriate adjustment studies (Black, Gregersen & Mendenhall 1992; Harvey 1997; Hippler 2000; Kulkarni, Lengnick-Hall & Valk, 2010; Mendenhall et al, 2008). As such, it was clearly of relevance to non-domestic transitions, whereas other models, noticeably that of Nicholson, were more centred on domestic transitions. Thirdly, in contrast to Nicholson's model, Louis' model is not primarily focussed on organisational transition. Since the migrant workers in this study were not transitioning between or within organisations, it was felt that Louis' model would allow for more flexibility in the study of their transitions.

One aspect of the interviewees' frustration at being overeducated was expressed as a determination to show their employers that they were willing to learn, flexible and efficient in the hope of being singled out as worthy of more responsibility. In some cases (Edmund, Sofija) this resulted in their being appointed to higher positions. However, others (Andrzej, Stanislaw) were not successful. Their accounts suggest that their employers did not welcome such visible demonstrations of potential from people in unskilled posts. Potentially, such failure to recognise and even resist such employee potential leads to a loss of potential talent for employers, as was argued by Felker (2011) in her recent study of educated migrants in the UK.

Another coping technique was to invest in training in order to make oneself more employable. Whereas the majority of the interviewees attended English classes, four of them paid for vocational or educational courses. In addition, both Isabella and Sebastian had come to the UK in order to raise money to fund their studies. Brigita, who was enrolled on a vocational conversion course in the hope of practising as a GP, also took on unpaid voluntary work to enhance her CV. Such efforts support the argument of the Neoclassical Economics theorists that migrants are willing to incur certain costs in order to invest in themselves with the intention of subsequently obtaining more profitable employment (Arango, 2000). To what extent their accumulation of human capital brought about by their attendance on such courses effectively allows them to subsequently escape from situations of skill- and status- underemployment is, however, beyond the scope of this study.

Clark & Drinkwater (2010) cite the high proportion of migrants who, dissatisfied with the work opportunities open to them, set themselves up as self employed. Although Celine worked freelance for a while and Edmund and Marjanna briefly toyed with the idea of becoming self-employed, only Pawel took this step. That he did so successfully implies that this is one avenue which migrants could explore. To what extent this benefits the drive towards a more mobile EU workforce, equipped to learn new skills and adapt to new environments in order to meet the EU's growth and jobs strategy (Vandenbrande et al, 2006) is open to question, however. As Clark & Drinkwater (2010) argued, however, if governments and other official bodies set up schemes which encourage migrant workers to set themselves up as self-employed, many do so. However, self employed migrants do not always utilise their qualifications and experience in their chosen business venture - Pawel was qualified to teach but was not allowed to teach in the UK. However, he was unqualified as a decorator, yet was able to set himself up in business as such. The clear implication is that governments and other official bodies may like to consider the possibility of utilising migrants' existing skills and qualifications by setting up schemes which encourage them to set themselves up as self employed within their existing area of expertise.

Nonwork adjustment

The fourth research question asked how nonwork and family factors affected the interviewees' adjustment to living and working in the UK. In contrast to the attention given to work adjustment in the expatriation literature, far less attention has been given to nonwork or general lifestyle adjustment practices in the host country (Grinstein & Wathieu, 2008; Andreason, 2008). However, Black, Mendenhall & Oddou (1991) stressed the need to take into consideration expatriates' experiences in adjusting to non-work activities affecting daily life in the new setting in areas such as living and housing conditions, food, health care, and the cost of living.

The interviewees' ability to adjust to their nonwork situation was affected not only by their lack of contact with educated native speakers (Spencer et al., 2007) but also by the lack of empathy with less educated locals (Trevena, 2009). Irregular or antisocial working hours, often in gruelling rotating shifts, also had a negative impact on their nonwork adjustment. Living among themselves or sharing with other migrants with whom they do not really get along, may marginalise the migrants and serve to restrict their personal development. Jiri and Valeska, for example, both in their fifties, lived ever more reclusive lives as they shunned other migrants. They had also both left their spouses in the home country, which had an impact on their general adjustment. This study does not have the scope to allow us to study older couples who decide that one of them should seek work overseas. However, this would appear to be a viable topic for future study.

Another factor a migrant has to take into consideration is whether his or her significant others, here or back home, are being negatively affected by his or her sojourn here. Brigita and Gabriela, for example, both saw huge benefits for their children in being here and this had a strong influence on their decision not to leave. In some cases, this led to friends and family joining the migrants here in the UK. Gabriela and Veronika were joined by their parents and siblings. Stanislaw invited Sebastian, a lifelong friend, to stay with him.

In common with studies of Poles in the UK (Trevena, 2006; Currie, 2006; Drinkwater, Eade & Garapich, 2006) the Polish interviewees distanced themselves from their less educated countrymen and felt little affinity to the earlier wave of Polish post war migrants. This dislike of one's compatriots seemed less marked among the other nationalities. Brigita was active within the local Lithuanian community, for example. As pointed out by Cook, Dwyer & White (2011), more research is needed into the interactions between different national groups of A8 migrants.

Transitioners are also faced with the need for relationship building. This straddles the work and nonwork fields. Several interviewees (Juliana and Ricardo, Stanislaw, Andrzej, Sebastian, Kamal, Veronika) pointed out the tense nature of their relationship with their superiors. In an attempt to alleviate such relationships, most interviewees made clear attempts to improve their English language skills. Those who were among the most successful in transitioning on to new and more suitable jobs (Sofija, Veronika, Pawel) felt that their high level of English was a main factor in this success.

Key findings

The examination of the motives of the interviewees in deciding to come to the UK to seek work reveal a complexity of factors in each individual's set of transitions. Louis (1980)'s distinction between the objective external differences (changes) and subjective internal reactions (contrasts) in transitions helped to highlight the importance of subjective factors in the analysis of how migrants reacted to the challenges experienced during their transition. Such factors help to explain why individuals' perceptions of concrete changes may vary, causing them to react in different ways to similar experiences. The individuality of the experiences which migrants face helps to explain the difficulty of classifying migrants into categories.

One more reason why the study finds it impracticable to categorise migrants into typologies lies in the longitudinal nature of their experiences. The cross–sectional nature of studies such as this one render attempts to classify migrants based on pre-existing categories difficult to apply. The fact that they continue to experience transitional pressures throughout their stay here makes it hard to justify attempts to place them into typologies based on intentions at the point of departure, or based on the situation in which they find themselves at the point of interview. Rather, their complex and evolving transitions demand a longitudinal examination since their strategic choices may shift as new experiences affect them and new opportunities present themselves, or fail to present themselves.

In common with previous studies of A8 migrants in the UK (Cook, Dwyer & Waite, 2011; Bell, Jarman & Lefebvre, 2004; Green, Owen and Jones, 2008; Schneider & Holman, 2009; McKay & Winkelmann-Gleed, 2005; Trevena, 2009), the analysis of the interviewees' motives revealed that financial factors were seen to be important but not exclusive. Several non-financial issues, particularly the desire to 'grow' and to learn and experience new things, were frequent factors mentioned for coming to the UK. The push /pull model (Lee, 1966) was a useful framework for the analysis of the various factors influencing migrants' in their decision as to whether or not to come to the UK. However, a distinction between the two sets of factors was seen to be less effective in real life situations, in which both push and pull factors tended to interact together.

A crucial factor in many of the migrants' accounts was the possibility of coming to the UK 'on spec' with the option of going back should the reality of life here not appeal. This was a direct consequence of the freedom of movement the migrants were granted in 2004. The ability to 'give it a go' without irrevocably leaving one's homeland behind is in stark contrast to many migration studies, especially those of forced migration. This freedom of movement further blurs the line between 'self-initiated expatriates' and 'migrants', since it grants the second group discernment in their decision.

The overeducation and underemployment literature provided a basis for the examination of the mismatch between the interviewees' qualifications and experience and the menial nature of the jobs they took on. In common with previous studies (e.g. Lianos, 2007; Patrinos, 1997; Nielsen, 2007: Liversage, 2009; Bauder, 2003; Kler, 2006; Green, Kler and Leeves, 2007; Waddington, 2007; Battu & Sloane, 2002; OECD, 2006) of overeducation among migrants, several factors played a part in this deskilling. Firstly, the lack of English ability played a central role in ruling out jobs commensurate with the migrants' backgrounds. The interviewees were hindered in their attempts to improve their level of English. The antisocial hours that they worked prevented them from attending classes and the lack of contact with native speakers prevented them from putting any new linguistic knowledge into practice.

A second barrier was a reluctance by agencies to recognise their qualifications and an emphasis on 'people shortages' rather than 'skills shortages' (Pemberton, 2008). Given the drive by the European Commission for Employment, Social Affairs and Equal Opportunities for a skilled mobile workforce (Vandenbrande et al., 2006), there would appear to be a need for high-level discussions around the harmonisation and accreditation of academic qualifications throughout the EU nation states.

The third barrier was a lack of funds with which to support lengthy job searches. The study's findings suggest that migrants may underestimate the difficulty of finding work commensurate with their level. This is aggravated by a relative lack of research into the labour market prior to departure from the home country (Felker, 2011).

An examination of the ways in which migrants coped with the skill- and status- underemployment in which they found themselves highlighted an area which has not received much attention in the literature. The effect of the migrants' downward transitions on their self esteem and sense of identity has only recently been the focus of studies (e.g. Trevena, 2010; Zikic et al, 2010). Despite the cross-sectional nature of the present study, some insight was gained into how the interviewees coped with such downward transitions.

One such method adopted was to strive to project an image as an exceptional employee. This involved spending their own money on training to enhance their desirability to current employers but also on courses which would help them to grow and settle, such as postgraduate degrees and English Language classes. Such attempts to obtain work more commensurate with their qualifications and experience whilst trapped in menial jobs helped them to narrow the gap between their self perceptions and looking glass selves (Trevena, 2006).

Even in such a small sample, there was evidence of planned and actual attempts to set themselves up as self employed in order to avoid job dissatisfaction (Clark & Drinkwater, 2010) although this route may not enable them to utilise their qualifications and experience fully. However, when given the opportunity to work on a freelance basis in areas which did utilise their skills, such as interpreting, the boost this gave to their self image was offset by their desire for permanent work, even when this was of a menial nature.

Within the expatriate adjustment literature, the ways in which expatriates adjust to nonwork has generally received less attention than the ways in which they adjust to work (Grinstein & Wathieu, 2008; Andreason, 2008). This study highlighted some aspects of the interviewees' nonwork adjustment, showing them to be marginalised. They avoided contact with UK nationals, whom they felt to be on a lower social level than themselves, with non-educated A8 migrants, whom they found embarrassing and disgusting, and often had quasi-racist attitudes towards ethnic minorities, of whose existence they had been unaware prior to arrival in the UK and whom they often struggled to accept.

The multi-faceted nature of human migration makes it necessary to address several literatures in order to address the complexity of the phenomenon. To this end, this study has contributed to the wider mobility literature; the literature on expatriation, especially self-initiated expatriation; the careers literature, especially the literature on international careers and that dealing with career transitions and 'new careers', and the literature on under-employment of highly-skilled workers. It has also adopted a European lens into the examination of EU-specific aspects of the mobility of skilled individuals and the implications of these.

It has done so from a qualitative and emic approach which resonates with recent studies into the reasons why people choose to migrate (e.g. Trevena, 2008; Anderson et al, 2006; Eade, Drinkwater, & Garapich, 2007). By focussing on the migrants' own experiences and interpretation of their decision to migrate and their subsequent experiences, it has enabled their personal experiences, aspirations, feelings and responses - which do not lend themselves easily to measurement - to be considered. By so doing it answers the call for more qualitative research into migration within Europe (de Tona, 2006).

The narratives of the interviewees in the study have highlighted the complex and interwoven factors which affect their decision to come to the UK in the hope of finding work. Despite the relatively rapid surge of research studies into the experiences of A8 migrants since accession in 2004 (e.g. McKay & Winkelmann-Gleed, 2005; Anderson et al, 2006; Currie, 2007; Drinkwater, Eade, & Garapich, 2006; Trevena, 2006; Felker, 2011), there is still scope for more research into their motivations for coming and experiences whilst here (Felker, 2011).

This study, in contrast to many other studies into A8 migrants in the UK (e.g. Trevena, 2006; 2010; Garapich 2008, Currie, 2006), did not restrict itself to a single national group. By widening the focus of the research to citizens of several countries, it has addressed the call by Cook, Dwyer & White (2011:73) to resist the urge to "homogenise the experiences of different nationalities and ethnic groups who make up the A8 migrant category". The inclusion in the sample of migrants from different countries helps to identify wider, non-nation specific, factors in their transitions. This is of particular importance given the planned further expansion of the EU and the possible opening up of the UK labour market to members of other current and future EU nation states.

The study adds to an understanding of new forms of international working (Mayrhofer, Sparrow, & Zimmermann, 2008) by shedding light on the experiences of a growing group of internationally mobile EU citizens. These individuals do not undertake the "one-off" movements typically studied in the migration literature since they are able, as a result of the freedom of movement which they enjoy as EU citizens, to undertake more fluid mobility between EU nation states (Piracha & Vickerman, 2002; Pennix et al., 2008). The focus on the European context addresses the need for a better understanding of contemporary career mobility within the EU (Khapova, Vinkenburg & Arnold, 2009; Mayrhofer & Schneidhofer, 2009). Such an understanding is vital if the community's ideals of a more mobile workforce, equipped to learn new skills and adapt to new environments and so able to increase the community's competitive ability in the face of growing globalisation (Vandenbrande et al., 2006; The European Foundation for the Improvement of Living and Working Conditions, 2006) are to be realised. Failure to harness effectively the skills and experiences of the EU workforce as a result of a lack of understanding of their needs would detract from this aim.

Interest in international career mobility research has centred on the experiences of corporate expatriates (Zikic et al, 2010; Carr, Inkson, & Thorn, 2005; Lee, 2005; Richardson, 2003; Thomas, Lazarova, & Inkson, 2005). Consequently, less is known about 'self-initiated expatriates', who form a much larger proportion of those working overseas than those who are sent overseas by their Multinational Corporation employers (Bonache, Brewster, & Suutari, 2001; Carr, Inkson, & Thorn, 2005; Inkson et al, 1997; Lee, 2005). By examining the motivations and experiences of A8 migrants who independently seek work in the United Kingdom, the present study helps to build on Richardson's (2003) call for more research into individuals who expatriate without organisational support or involvement. By examining a group of individuals who straddle the groups of 'self-initiated expatriates' and 'migrants/migrant workers', the study broadens the scope of the relatively new existing literature on self-initiated expatriates (e.g. Richardson, 2003; 2006; Froese, 2011; Felker, 2011) and links this literature with that on A8 migrants and migrant workers. This is also a recent topic of study since accession to the A8 countries was only granted in 2004. The present study therefore sheds light on two growing and recent areas of study by highlighting similarities and differences between the two groups of 'self-initiated expatriates' and 'migrants/migrant workers'.

Recent studies of careers have focussed on individuals' ability to take advantage of changes in the economic and organisational landscape in order to proactively take charge of their own 'boundaryless careers' (Arthur and Rousseau, 1996). Such careers have evolved, it is argued, in contrast to traditional organizational careers carried out in a single employment setting. Not only organisational boundaries, but also geographical, role and professional ones and even subjective ones are crossed. Arthur and

Rousseau's (1996) rhetoric of skilled individuals exercising agency and mobility in Silicon Valley chimes in nicely with the vision proposed by the European Foundation for the Improvement of Living and Working Conditions (2006) of a more mobile EU-wide workforce, equipped to learn new skills and adapt to new environments in order to meet the community's growth and jobs strategy.

And yet the narratives of the migrant workers interviewed in this study do not resonate with Arthur and Rousseau's (1996) picture of personal empowerment and ease of adaptation to a new situation. Instead, their stories cause us to question whether the fruits of their boundary crossing are not the joy of free agency and having charge over their careers but rather insecurity, underemployment and anxiety. This study suggests that after they have crossed boundaries to seek work here, other boundaries present themselves to thwart their ambitions and cause us to question the appropriateness of the boundaryless careers theory in the European Community of the 21st Century, which would have appeared to have been an ideal environment for such boundaryless careers to thrive in.

Another contribution is the explicit examination of the skill- and status-underemployment brought about by taking on jobs which are not commensurate with skilled migrants' qualifications and experience. 'Overeducated' migrants are unable to take up jobs for which they are qualified and consequently the UK does not benefit fully from their talents and experience (Waddington, 2007; Pemberton, 2008). However, less attention has been given to the psychological effect of overeducation and skill- and status- related underemployment on migrants, despite the frequent reports of migrants working in jobs not commensurate with their skills and qualifications (e.g. Lianos, 1997; Currie, 2006, Trevena, 2006; Liversage, 2009; Felker, 2011; Schneider & Holman, 2005). Their inability to find work commensurate with their skills and experience could have adverse effects on their mental health (Dooley, Prause & Ham-Rowbottom, 2000; Friedland & Price, 2003; Dean & Wilson, 2009) and may detract from their ability to integrate fully into wider UK society (Waddington, 2007; Trevena, 2008).

An understanding of the effect that skilled migrants' skill- and status-underemployment has on them helps to alert government bodies and professional associations to the threat of such potential problems. It highlights the need to pay attention to the potential negative effects of overeducation and skill- and status- underemployment in order to prevent possible marginalization of migrant workers and potential subsequent social tensions. By understanding the difficulties which the interviewees face as a result of the skill- and status- underemployment in which they find themselves, such organisations could proactively put measures – such as free

English language programmes at suitable times and expedited recognition schemes for non-UK based qualifications – in place before problems occur.

Traditionally, studies of "skilled migrants" utilise a narrow, academic concept of skill - the holding of a degree (GCIM, 2005). This study challenges this restriction, arguing that the concept of skill should be extended to cover a much wider view of the possession of specialist knowledge, including technical and vocational knowledge. This suggests that the negative effects of skill- and status- underemployment are potentially more widespread than the literature to date has assumed. It raises the question as to whether recognition schemes for non-academic qualifications within the EU can be improved so that migrants with specialised but non-academic skills are able to obtain jobs within their field of specialisation. Such lack of recognition of qualifications obtained in other EU nation states is not restricted to the UK but is widespread throughout the community (Barone, 2009). Until such time as a community-wide recognition scheme is operational, the full integration of suitably qualified and experienced individuals into the workplace in other nation states within the community will be hindered.

By restricting its focus to individuals who are in jobs which are not commensurate with their qualifications and experience, the study helps to add to the relatively small body of knowledge on individuals in skill- and status-underemployment undergoing voluntary (i.e. unforced) downward transitions. The motives of those who accept work below their level of qualifications and experience has received scant attention in the literature (Slay, 2006; Newman, 1999; Rooth & Ekberg, 2006; Remennick, 1999; Miller, Haskell, & Thatcher, 2002). Individuals undergoing such transitions in their home country, possibly as a consequence of demotion or redundancy, face an added layer of complexity as they need to come to terms with the differences between their old and new status, since status affects both social interaction and self-verification (Stryker & Burke, 2000; Sargent, 2003).

Those who do so in a new country are faced with three types of transition – a physical transition between countries, a psychological transition between cultures and a status transition between old and new professional and social standing. Transition models such as Louis (1980) and Nicholson (1984; 1990), whilst addressing domestic downward transitions, fail to account for the complexity of the transitions facing those undergoing international downward transitions. One key failing of such models is their inability to account for the possibility of withdrawal – i.e. return to the home country or migration to a third country. Given the freedom of movement enjoyed by EU citizens who find themselves in a new country in a situation of skill- and status- underemployment, such an exit strategy is very real. This study lays the first foundation stones towards the construction of a model which would combine the insights gained from the domestic transition literature (Louis, 1980; Nicholson, 1984; 1990) with the specific needs of such EU migrant workers.

Finally, the study offers, in addition to its theoretical contribution to the field of careers transition literature, a potential tool for those considering migrating within the European Union, or for those whose task it is to assist these people to adjust to their new lives, with which to track and manage their transitions. It identifies key areas to which they need to pay attention both before and during the move to the UK.

Suggestions for further research

The results of this study suggest some new areas for further research. Firstly, given the differences between individuals, there would appear to be a need for research to reduce the granularity of the lens through which 'migrants' are viewed. Liversage (2009) highlights the drawbacks of relying on aggregated groups of migrants rather than individuals and argues for a more individual approach to examining their experiences. Attempts to establish a 'migrant personality' (Boneva and Frieze, 2001) also help to shift the focus from the group to the individual. Research into how such personality traits affect migrants' transitions not just before departure but also after arrival, may help to present a more focussed picture of migrants' individual lived experiences.

Secondly, there has been a paucity of studies which have attempted to apply models from the domestic relocation literature to the study of overseas transitions, despite the suggestion by Nicholson that his 1984 model could:

*"... with minor conceptual modification .. yield predictions about the outcomes of retirement, redundancy, reemployment, **geographical migration**, and other life-space transitions." (Nicholson, 1984:188 - emphasis added).*

There is scope for further studies which apply such models to the analysis of transitions across national and cultural boundaries. Such models would need to take account of the potential negative effects of skill- and status-underemployment on migrant workers as well as the physical and psychological effects of their move.

Thirdly, there is a clear need for longitudinal studies in order to more clearly identify the motives for migrant workers' decisions to leave the UK. As Piracha and Vickerman (2002) point out, intra-European migration involves return and serial migration. Consequently, there is a need to study the subsequent moves of migrant workers who have left the UK. This applies whether they return to the UK or decide to move to other countries within the community in order to seek or take up work. Such longitudinal research would enable us to gain a more general overview of their motives, the barriers they face in finding suitable work, and the adjustment techniques they undergo. Over time, this would allow us to compare the challenges faced by migrants in different member states with different labour market provisions and state support for language courses (Liversage, 2009).

Fourthly, most previous studies (e.g. Trevena, 2008; Drinkwater, Eade & Garapich, 2006; Currie, 2006) have concentrated on Polish migrant workers. There is a clear need for more studies which examine the lived experiences of A8 migrants of different nationalities (Cook, Dwyer & White, 2011). Such studies may reveal commonalities and differences between migrants of different national groups, and shed light on the relationships, both work and nonwork, between them. Of especial interest would be an in-depth analysis of the experiences of dual nationality migrants of non-European origin (e.g. Brazilian/Portuguese; Brazilian/Italian) who, despite having an EU passport, are normally resident in a non-EU country.

Finally, although small-scale studies such as the present one are valuable in exploring new research areas, they can only hope to serve as an impetus for studies using larger samples. Several such large-scale studies into migrant workers in the United Kingdom have been conducted in the first decade of the 21st Century. However, these have tended to concentrate on aspects of their lives other than those presented by the model in the current study. The use of such studies to build on, confirm or refute some of the assertions in the present study would be welcomed.

Undoubtedly, the present study has a number of limitations, some related to the sample and others related to the design.

In common with many qualitative studies, the sample size was very small, and it would therefore be difficult to generalise the findings to the wider migrant population. A further limitation, also related to the sample, is that of its composition. This applies in two aspects: firstly, the sample was self-selected and therefore the views of the interviewees could have differed substantially from others in similar circumstances who were not interviewed. The decision to interview in English also possibly dissuaded some potential interviewees from agreeing to take part. Secondly, despite my best efforts in attempting to make the sample as diverse as possible (it was decided at an early stage not to interview a group of Poles living in the same house and working in the same factory), there is a certain imbalance in the backgrounds, linguistic prowess and prior overseas experiences of the interviewees. Each of these factors may have had effects on their adjustment to living and working in the UK which went unnoticed in their accounts.

It is naive to report on interviews which are conducted in a language other than the mother tongue of the interviewees as one would report on those conducted in the mother tongue (Temple & Young, 2004). Potential negative effects of the decision to interview in English include the possible exclusion of potential interviewees, the creation of a barrier between the interviewer and the interviewees leading to a lack of rapport and, therefore, possibly to a lack of openness on the part of the interviewees, and the possibility of linguistic or cultural misunderstandings in the interpretation of the interviewees.

Another significant limitation of the study is its cross-sectional nature. In the absence of a longitudinal study, it is impossible to ascertain whether the interviewees continued in their menial jobs, persevered with their quest for work, returned home or sought other UK work. A longitudinal study might have shed light on the factors which persuaded them to end their stay here.

Finally, the fact that I, and I alone, conducted, transcribed and analysed the interviews could lead to accusation of single-researcher bias. No concerted effort was undertaken, for example, to establish inter-coder agreement in the analysis stage. Also, the decision to interview in English may have affected my interpretation of some of the interviewees' comments, especially given the language constraints they were under.

In this book I have highlighted the complexity of the factors influencing the interviewees' decision to come to the UK. I believe that my own experiences have played a role in keeping me enthused for the topic I have chosen and the analysis presented in this book has benefited from that reflexive experience. Despite certain limitations, I believe that this study supplements the many recent studies of migrant workers in the UK by focusing on their lived experiences as seen through the lens of skill- and status- underemployment. It has shed light on the changes which my interviewees faced as a result of their decision to come to the UK to seek or take up work. The reality of their situation was very often at odds with their preconceptions. Since each individual's ability to adjust to such changes varies (Louis, 1980) and situations change over time, this study has just begun to examine the effects of working in jobs that are not commensurate with one's qualifications and experience. It is hoped that it will encourage further research to address these issues and by so doing benefit future generations of EU migrant workers.

Appendix 1: Interview guide

Tell me about yourself
Male or female?
Age?
Country of origin?
Marital Status?
How is your English? Speaking, listening, reading, writing?
What other languages do you speak?
 What is your educational background (age when left school, further/higher education, degrees obtained, where obtained etc.)
What professional qualifications do you have?
Is/are your professional qualification or degree recognised in England?
What job(s) did you do before coming to England?

Tell me about your family
Are you married/living with a partner?
Do you have children?
Are any family members with you here in the UK?
What are they doing here? (working, at school..???)
Do they plan to come later?
 If they are still in your home country, what are they doing there? (working, at school..???)
 How did they feel about your decision to come to the UK to work?
 How do you stay in touch with family members back in your home country?

Tell me why you came here.
What was your main reason for seeking work in the UK ?
Was this your first time in the UK ? (If not, tell me about the other times).
Were any of your friends or family members working in the UK when you decided to come? How did that influence you?
Did you arrange a job before you left your home country or once you had arrived here?
Tell me about your journey to England.
What were your first impressions of the UK?

Tell me about your job(s).
Have you registered with the Workers Registration Scheme?
Do you have a National Insurance Number?
Where are you working at the moment?
How long have you been working there?
How did you get this job?
 (if this is not your first job in the UK, or if you have other jobs as well, please tell me about the other jobs as well)
 What do you do in your job?

Describe a typical working day.

How does the job(s) you are doing utilize your educational and vocational qualifications? I mean do you need those qualifications to do it?

How does the job compare to your ideal job? To your jobs in your home country?

What do you like best about your job? Least?

Have you had any positive/negative experiences you would like to share with me?

Who would you turn to if you had a problem? Why?

How do you feel about the pay?

How do you feel you are treated compared to British workers?

How do you feel treated by your colleagues?

How long do you think you will stay in this job?

Why?

Tell me about your plans.

Are you doing any skills training / studying at the moment?

Why? Why not?

Do you have any plans to do vocational training or to study in the UK in the future?

How long do you plan to stay in the UK?

Where do you think you will you go after you leave? (back home or to another EU country?)

Where do you see yourself in 3 years time? 5 years? 10 years?

Tell me about your life outside of work

How did you find your accommodation?

Are you living on your own or with other people?

Have you had any difficulties with your accommodation?

Has it been easy to meet new people since coming to England?

Why? Why not?

Who do you spend time with?

Where are they from? How did you meet them?

What do you do in your free time?

What do you miss most about being away from your home country?

What do like most about the UK?

How do you think British people see you?

Have you had any positive/negative experiences you would like to share with me?

Who would you turn to if you had a problem? Why?

And finally

Looking back at your time in the UK, how would you evaluate your experiences here? What are the positive and negative themes and why?

References

Ackers, L. (2004). Managing relationships in peripatetic careers: Scientific mobility in the European Union. *Women's Studies International Forum*, 27, 189-201.

Adamson, S. J., Doherty, N. & Viney, C. (1998). The Meanings of Career Revisited: Implications for Theory and Practice. *British Journal of Management*, 9, 251-259.

Ainsaar, M. (2004). *Reasons for move: A study on trends and reasons of internal migration with particular interest in Estonia, 1989--2000* (Vol. Ph.D.). Ph.D. thesis, University of Turku

Al Ariss, A. (2010). Modes of Engagement: Migration, Self-Initiated Expatriation, and Career Development. *Career Development International*, 15(4), 338 - 358

Ali, M. (2003) *Brick Lane*. London: Black Swan.

Anderson, B. and Rogaly, B. (2005). *Forced Labour and Migration to the UK*, London: Trades Union Congress in association with Centre for Migration, Policy and Society (COMPAS), University of Oxford

Anderson, B., Ruhs, M., Rogaly, B. and Spencer, S. (2006). Fair Enough? Central and East European Migrants in Low-Wage Employment In The UK, York: Joseph Rowntree Foundation.

Andreason, A.W. (2008). Expatriate adjustment of spouses and expatriate managers: an integrative research review. *International Journal of Management*, 25, 382-395.

Appleyard, R. (1989). *The Impact of International Migration on Developing Countries*. Paris,: OECD.

Arango, J. (2000). Explaining Migration: A Critical View. *International Social Science Journal*, 52, 283-296.

Arber, S. (1993). The Research Process. In N. Gilbert. (ed.) (1993) *Researching Social Life*. London, California, New Delhi: Sage Publications, pp. 32-50

Arnold, J. (1997). *Managing Careers into the 21st Century*, London: Paul Chapman

Arnold, J. & Cohen, L. (2008). The Psychology of Careers in Industrial and Organizational Settings: A Critical but Appreciative Analysis. *International Review of Industrial and Organizational Psychology*, 23, 1-44.

Arthur M.B., Hall D.T. and Lawrence B.S. (1989). Generating new directions in career theory: The case for a transdisciplinary approach. In: Arthur MB, Hall DT and Lawrence BS (eds) The Handbook of Career Theory. Cambridge: Cambridge University Press, 7-25.

Arthur, M. B., & Rousseau, D. M. (1996). The boundaryless career as a new employment principle. In M. G. Arthur & D. M. Rousseau (Eds.), *The boundaryless career*. New York: Oxford University Press, 3–20

Arthur, M.B. & Lawrence, B.S. (1984). Perspectives on environment and career: An introduction. *Journal of Organizational Behavior*, 5, 1-8.

Arthur, M. B., Khapova, S. N. & Wilderom, C. P. M. (2005). Career success in a boundaryless career world. *Journal of Organizational Behavior*, 26 (2): 177-202

Ashforth, B.E. (2001). Role transitions in organizational life: an identity-based perspective, Mahwah, Lawrence Erlbaum, Inc.

Audit Commission (2007). *Crossing borders: Responding to the local challenges of migrant workers.* London: The Audit Commission.

Aycan, Z. (1997). Acculturation of expatriate managers: A process model of adjustment and performance. In Z. Aycan (Ed.), *New approaches to employee management*, 4, pp. 1-40

Balter, M. (1999). Europeans who do postdocs abroad face re-entry problems. *Science*, 3, 1524-1526.

Barley, S.R. (1989). Careers, identities, and institutions: the legacy of the Chicago School of Sociology.

Barone, C. and European Foundation for the Improvement of Living and Working Conditions (Eurofound). (2009). Occupational promotion of migrant workers. Dublin, Ireland. Available online at: http://www.eurofound.europa.eu/docs/ewco/tn0807038s /tn0807038s.pdf [Accessed 25 January, 2010].

Baruch, Y. (2004). Transforming careers: from linear to multidirectional career paths: Organizational and individual perspectives. *Career Development International*, 9, 58-73.

Baruch, Y. & Rosenstein, E. (1992). Career Planning and Managing in High Tech Organizations. *International Journal of Human Resource Management*, 3, 477-496.

Bateson, M.C. (1989) *Composing a Life*, New York, Atlantic Monthly Press.

Battu, H. & Sloane, P.J. (2002).To what extent are ethnic minorities in Britain overeducated? *International Journal of Manpower*, 23, 192-208.

Bauder, H. (2003). "Brain abuse", or the devaluation of immigrant labour in Canada. *Antipode*, 35, 699-717.

Bauer, T.K., Haisken-DeNew, J.P. & Schmidt, C.M. (2004). *International Labor Migration, Economic Growth and Labor Markets. The Current State of Affairs.* Essen,: RWI: Discussion Papers No. 20.

Bell, K., Jarman, N. & Lefebvre, T. (2004). *Migrant Workers in Northern Ireland.*, Belfast, ICR.

Benson-Rea, M. & Rawlinson, S. (2003). Highly Skilled and Business Migrants: Information Processes and Settlement Outcomes, *International Migration*, 41:2, 59-79

Berry J. W. (1997). Immigration, acculturation, and adaptation. *Applied Psychology: An International Review, 46,* 5-34.

Berry, J. W. (1992). Acculturation and adaptation in a new society. *International Migration Review, 30,* 69-85.

Berry, J.W., Kim, U., Minde, T. & Mok, D. (1987). Comparative studies of acculturative stress. *International Migration Review*, 21, 491-511

Bhaskar-Shrinivas P., Harrison D.A., Luk D.M., Shaffer M.A. (2005). Input-based and time-based models of international adjustment: meta-analytic evidence and theoretical extensions. *Academy of Management Journal*, 48:2, 57–81

Biernacki P. & Waldorf D. (1981). Snowball sampling: problem and techniques of chain referral sampling. *Sociological Methods and Research* 10:2, 141–163

Bishop, J.H. (1993). Overeducation (CAHRS Working Paper 93-06), Ithaca, NY: Cornell University.

Black, J. S., Gregersen, H. B., & Mendenhall, M. E. (1992). Toward a theoretical framework of repatriation adjustment. *Journal of International Business Studies*, 23(4), 737-754.

Black, J.S. (1988). Work Role Transitions: A Study of American Expatriate Managers in Japan. *Journal of International Business Studies*, 19, 277-294.

Black, J.S., Mendenhall, M. & Oddou, G. (1991). Toward a comprehensive model of international adjustment: an integration of multiple theoretical perspectives. *Academy of Management Review*, 16, 291-318.

Blau, G. (2000). Job, organizational, and professional context antecedents as predictors of intent for interrole work transitions. *Journal of Vocational Behavior*, 56(3), 330-345.

Bonache, J., Brewster, C. & Suutari, V. (2001). Expatriation: a developing research agenda. *Thunderbird International Business Review*, 43, 3-20.

Boneva, B.S. & Frieze, I.H. (2001). Toward a Concept of a Migrant Personality. *Journal of Social Issues*, 57, 477-491.

Borjas, G.J. (1994). The Economics of Immigration. *Journal of Economic Literature*, 32, 1667-1717.

Bourdieu, P. & Wacquant., L.J.D. (1992). *An Invitation to Reflexive Sociology*. Chicago: University of Chicago Press.

Bourhis, R. Y., Moïse, L. C., Perreault, S., & Senécal, S. (1997). Towards an Interactive acculturation Model: a social psychological approach. *International Journal of Psychology*, 32, 369-386

Boyd, M. (1989). Family and Personal Networks in International Migration: Recent Developments and New Agendas. *International Migration Review*, 23, 638-670.

Brandi, M.C. (2001). Skilled Immigrants in Rome. *International Migration*, 39, 101-131.

Breakwell, G.M. (1983). *Threatened identities*. Chichester: Wiley.

Brinkmann, S., & Kvale, S. (2005). Confronting the ethics of qualitative research, *Journal of Constructivist Psychology*, 18(2), 157-181.

Brocklehurst, M. (2003). Self and place: a critique of the boundaryless career, paper presented to the Critical Management Studies Conference, University of Lancaster, Lancaster

Brown, G. & Pintaldi, F. (2006). A multidimensional approach in the measurement of underemployment. *Statistical Journal of the United Nations Economic Commission for Europe*, 23, 43-56.

Bruce, R. A., & Scott, S. G. (1994). Varieties and commonalities of career transitions: Louis' typology revisited. *Journal of Vocational Behavior*, 45: 17-40.

Bryman, A. (2004). *Social Research Methods*. Oxford: Oxford University Press.

bSolutions, (2005). *An Initial Survey of Migrant Labour in the North East of Scotland*, Scotland: Banff & Buchan College of Further Education.

Burris, B.H. (1983). The human effects of underemployment. *Social Problems*, 31, 96-110.

Butler-Kisber, L. & Poldma, T. (2009). *The power of visual approaches in qualitative inquiry: The use of collage making and concept mapping in experiential research*. Experiential Knowledge, Method & Methodology.

International Conference of the DRS Special Interest Group on Experiential Knowledge. Canada, 19 June 2009

Carling, J. (2002). Migration in the Age of Involuntary Immobility: Theoretical Reflections and Cape Verdean Experiences. *Journal of Ethnic and Migration Studies*, 28, 5-42.

Carr, S.C., Inkson, K. & Thorn, K. (2005). From global careers to talent flow: Reinterpreting 'brain drain'. *Journal of World Business*, 40, 386-398.

Castles, S. (2000). International migration at the beginning of the twenty-first century: global trends and issues. *International Social Science Journal*, 52:165, 269-281.

Castles, S. (2003). 'Towards a sociology of forced migration and social transformation', *Sociology,* 37(1) :13-34.

Castles S, Miller M.J. (2003). *The Age of Migration*. Houndmills, Basingstoke, Hampshire and London: MacMillan Press Ltd

Chiswick, B. & Miller, P.W. (2009). The international transferability of immigrants' human capital, *Economics of Education Review.* 28, pp. 162–169

Clark, K, & Drinkwater, S. (2010). Recent trends in minority ethnic entrepreneurship in Britain. *International Small Business Journal.* 28 (2), 136-146.

Clogg, C.C., Eliason, S.R. & Wahl, R.J. (1990). Labor-market experiences and labor-force outcomes. *American Journal of Sociology*, 95, 1536-1576.

Clogg, C.C., Sullivan, T.A. & Mutchler, J.E. (1986). Measuring Underemployment and Inequality in the Work Force. *Social Indicators Research*, 18, 375-393.

Coffey, A., Holbrook, B. & Atkinson, P. (1996). Qualitative Data Analysis: Technologies and Representations, *Sociological Research Online,* vol. 1, no. 1, Available: http://www.socresonline.org.uk/1/1/4.html [Accessed 14 March, 2007].

Cohen L. and Mallon M. (2001). My brilliant career? Using stories as a methodological tool in careers research. *International Studies of Management and Organization* 31:3, 48-68.

Cohen, J. H. and Sirkeci, I. (2011). *Cultures of migration: The global nature of contemporary mobility.* Austin, TX, USA: University of Texas Press.

Collin, A. & Young, R. A. (2000). The future of career. In: A. Collin & R. A. Young (Eds), *The future of career*, Cambridge: Cambridge University Press, 276-300.

Collis, J. and Hussey, R. (2003). *Business research,* Basingstoke: Palgrave

Congdon, P. (2008). Models for Migration Age Schedules: A Bayesian Perspective with an Application to Flows between Scotland and England In J. Raymer & F. Willekens (Eds), *International Migration in Europe: Data, Models and Estimates.* Chichester: Wiley; 2008, 193-205

Cook, J., Dwyer, P. and Waite, L. (2011). The Experiences of Accession 8 Migrants in England: Motivations, Work and Agency, *International Migration*, 49: 54–79

Cooley, C. H., (1902). Human Nature and the Social Order. New York, Transaction

CRC. (2007). *A8 migrant workers in rural areas: a briefing paper.* Cheltenham: Commission for Rural Communities.

Currie, S. (2006). Free Movers? The Post-Accession Experience of Accession-8 Migrant Workers in the UK. *European Law Review*, 31, 207-229.

Currie, S. (2007). De-Skilled and Devalued: The Labour Market Experience of Polish Migrants in the UK Following EU Enlargement. *International Journal of Comparative Labour Law and Industrial Relations*, 83-116.

Datta, K., McIlwaine, C., Evans, Y., Herbert, J., May J., and Wills, J. (2007). From Coping Strategies to Tactics: London's Low-Pay Economy and Migrant Labour, *British Journal of Industrial Relations*, 45:2, pp. 404–432

De Jong, G., Chamratrithirong, A., & Tran, Q. (2002). For better, for worse: Life satisfaction consequences of migration in Thailand. International Migration Review, 36, 838–863

De Lima, P., Jentsch, B., and Whelton R. (2005). Migrant Workers in the Highlands and Islands, Report for Highlands and Islands Enterprise by UHI PolicyWeb

De Tona, C. (2006). "But what is interesting is the story of why and how migration happened". Ronit Lentin and Hassan Bousetta in conversation with Carla De Tona. Available online at: http://nbn-resolving.de/urn:nbn:de:0114-fqs0603139 [Accessed 20 August, 2008]

Dean, J.A. & Wilson, K. (2009). 'Education? It is irrelevant to my job now. It makes me very depressed…' Exploring the health impacts of under/unemployment among highly skilled recent immigrants in Canada. *Ethnicity and Health*, 14, 185-204

Dench, S., Hurstfield, J., Hill, D., Akroyd, K. (2006). Employers' Use of Migrant Labour. Main Report, Home Office Online Report 04/06. Available: http://www.homeoffice.gov.uk/rds/pdfs06/rdsolr0406.pdf. [Accessed 23 February, 2008]

Denscombe, M. (2007). *The Good Research Guide: for small-scale social research* (third edition). Maidenhead: Open University Press.

Denzin, N.K. (1989). *The Research Act: A Theoretical Introduction to Sociological Methods* Englewood Cliffs, NJ, Prentice-Hall.

Denzin, N.K. (1992). *Symbolic interactionism*. Newbury Park, CA:: Sage.

Denzin, N.K. & Lincoln, Y.S. (1994). "Introduction: Entering the field of qualitative research." In N.K. Denzin and Y.S. Lincoln (eds.) Handbook of Qualitative Research. Thousand Oaks: Sage, 1-18

Dey, I. (1993). *Qualitative data analysis: A user-friendly guide*. London: Routledge.

Dickinson, S.; Thompson, G.; Prabhakar, M.; Hurstfield, J.; Doel, C.. (2008). *Migrant workers Economic Issues and Opportunities*. SQW Consulting. Available: www.sqw.co.uk/file_download/133 [Accessed 15 December, 2009]

Dolton, P. & Vignoles, A. (2000). The incidence and effects of overeducation in the U.K. graduate labour market. *Economics of Education Review*, 19, 179-198.

Dooley, D., Prause, J., & Ham-Rowbottom, K. A. (2000). Underemployment and depression: Longitudinal relationships. *Journal of Health and Social Behavior*, 41, 421–436.

Drinkwater, S. (2003). Go West? Assessing the Willingness to Move from Central and Eastern European Countries. *Unpublished paper, Department of Economics, University of Surrey, UK*

Drinkwater, S., Eade, J., Garapich, M. (2006). Poles Apart? EU Enlargement and the Labour Market Outcomes of Immigrants in the UK. IZA Discussion Paper No. 2410, Bonn.

Dumont, J.-C. and G. Lemaitre (2005). Counting immigrants and expatriates in OECD countries, *OECD Social, Employment and Migration Working Papers* No. 25, OECD, Paris

Dustmann, C. & Fabbri, F. (2003). Language Proficiency and Labour Market Performance of Immigrants In The UK. *The Economic Journal*, 113, 695-717.

Duvell, F. & Vogel, D. (2006). Polish Migrants: Tensions between Sociological Typologies and State Categories. In A. Triandafyllidou, (Ed) *Contemporary Polish Migration in Europe: Complex Patterns of Movement and Settlement,* Edwin Mellen Press, New York, 267-289.

Eade J, Drinkwater, S.J., Garapich M. (2007). *Class and Ethnicity: Polish Migrants in London.* Economic and Social Research Council End of Award Report, RES-000-22-1294, Available: http://www.surrey.ac.uk/cronem/files/POLISH_FINAL_RESEARCH _REPORT_WEB.pdf [Accessed: 19 January, 2007]

Easterby-Smith, M., Thorpe, R. and Lowe, A. (2002). *Management Learning: an Introduction,* London: Sage

Ebaugh, H.R.F. (1988). *Becoming an Ex: The process of role exit.* Chicago, University of Chicago Press Chicago: University of Chicago Press.

European Commission (2013) Modernisation of the Professional Qualifications Directive – frequently asked questions Available: http://europa.eu/rapid/press-release_MEMO-13-867_en.htm [Accessed 10 October, 2015)

Evans, Y., Herbert, J., Datta, K., May, J., McIlwaine, C. and Wills, J. (2005). *Making the City Work: Low paid employment in London.* Department of Geography, Queen Mary, University of London

Faist, T., (1997). The Crucial Meso-Level. in: T. Hammar, G. Brochmann, K. Tamas and T. Faist (Eds.), *International Migration, Immobility and Development.* Oxford: Berg, 187–217

Faist T. (2000). *The Volume and Dynamics of International Migration and Transnational Social Spaces.* Clarendon Press: Oxford.

Favell, A. (2008). The New Face of East-West Migration in Europe. *Journal of Ethnic and Migration Studies*, 34, 701-716.

Fawcett, J.T., Arnold, F., (1987). The role of surveys in the study of international migration: an appraisal. *International Migration Review* 21 (4), 1523–1540.

Feldman, D.C. (1996). The Nature, Antecedents and Consequences of Underemployment. *Journal of Management*, 22:3, 385-407.

Felker, J. A. (2011). Professional development through self-directed expatriation: intentions and outcomes for young, educated Eastern Europeans, *International Journal of Training and Development*, 15(1), pp. 76-86

Felstead, A., Gallie, D. and Green, F. (2002). *Work skills in Britain 1986-2001.* London: Department for Education and Skills

Ferro, A. (2006). Desired mobility or satisfied immobility? Migratory aspirations among knowledge workers. *Journal of Education and Work*, 19, 171-200.

Fielding, N. G. and Lee, R. M. (eds) (1991). Using Computers in Qualitative Research, London: Sage.

Fielding N. G. (Ed.) (1993). *Researching Social Life*. Sage, London.

Fischer, P.A. & Malmberg, G. (2001). Settled people don't move: on life-course and (im)mobility in Sweden. *International Journal of Population Geography*, 7, 357-371.

Flatau, P., Petridis, R. & Wood, G. (1995) *Immigrants and Invisible Underemployment*. Canberra, Australian Government Publishing Service.

Fontana, A., & Prokos, A. H. (2007). *The interview: From formal to postmodern*. Walnut Creek, CA: Left Coast Press.

Forrier, A., Sels, L. & Stynen, D. (2009). Career mobility at the intersection between agent and structure: A conceptual model. *Journal of Occupational and Organizational Psychology*, 82:4, 739-759

Friedberg, R.M. (2000). You can't take it with you? Migrant assimilation and the portability of human capital. *Journal of Labour Economics*, 18, 221-251.

Friedland, D.S. & Price, R.H. (2003). Underemployment: Consequences for the health and well-being of workers. *American Journal of Community Psychology*, 32, 33-45.

Froese, F.J. (2011). Motivation and adjustment of self-initiated expatriates: The case of expatriate academics in South Korea. *International Journal of Human Resource Management.*, iFirst, DOI: 10.1080/09585192.2011.561220

Gans, H.J. (1999). Filling some holes: Six areas of needed immigration research. *American Behavioral Scientist*, 42, 1302-1313.

Garapich, M. (2008). The Migration Industry and Civil Society: Polish Immigrants in the United Kingdom before and after EU Enlargement, *Journal of Ethnic and Migration Studies* 34:5, 735-52.

Garnier, P. (2001). Foreign Workers from Central and Eastern European Countries in some OECD European Countries: Status and Social Protection. In OECD, (Ed) *Migration Policies and EU Enlargement: The Case of Central and Eastern Europe,* OECD, 131-154.

GCIM (2005). Migration in an Interconnected World: New Directions for Action, *GCIM*, Available: http://www.gcim.org/en/finalreport.html [Accessed 12 September, 2006]

Glanz, L., Williams, R., & Hoeksema, L. (2001). "Sensemaking in expatriation – a theoretical basis", *Thunderbird International Business Review*, Vol. 43 No.1, pp.101-19.

Goss, E. & Schoening, N.C. (1984). Search time, unemployment, and the migration decision. *Journal of Human Resources*, 19, 570-579.

Gowler, D. and Legge, K. (1989). Rhetoric in Bureaucratic Careers: managing the meaning of management success, in M. B. Arthur, D. T. Hall and B. S. Lawrence. (eds), *The Handbook of Career Theory*, Cambridge: Cambridge University Press.

Green, A., Owen, D. & Wilson, R. (2005). *Regional Profiles of the Workforce by Ethnicity and Migrant Workers: Regional Profiles (9 volumes)*. LSC.

Green, A.E, Owen, D. and Jones, P. (2008). Migrant Workers in the South East Regional Economy. Coventry, Institute of Employment Research, University of Warwick

Green, C.; Kler, P. and Leeves, G. (2007). "Immigrant overeducation: Evidence from recent arrivals to Australia", *Economics of Education Review* 26, pp. 420-432.

Greenwood, M.J. (1997). Internal migration in developed countries. In M.R. Rosenzweig & O. Stark (Eds) *Handbook of Population and Family Economics,* Elsevier, Amsterdam, 647-720.

Grinstein, A. and Wathieu, L., (2008). Cosmopolitanism, Assignment Duration, and Expatriate Adjustment: The Trade-Off between Well-Being and Performance, ESMT Working Paper No. 08-011. Available: http://ssrn.com/abstract=1353128 [Accessed June 9th, 2009]

Groot, W. (1996). The incidence of and returns to overeducation in the UK. *Applied Economics*, 28, 227-236.

Guba, E. G., & Lincoln, Y. S. (1994). Competing paradigms in qualitative research. In N. K. Denzin & Y. S. Lincoln (Eds.), Handbook of qualitative research (pp. 105-117). Thousand Oaks, CA: Sage

Hall, D.T. (1996). Protean Careers of the 21st Century. *Academy of Management Review*, 10, 8-16.

Hall, D.T. (2002). *Careers In and Out of Organizations*, Sage, Thousand Oaks, CA, .

Hammar, T. and Tamas, K. (1997). 'Why do people go or stay?', in Hammar, T., Brochmann, G., Tamas, K. and Faist, T. (eds) *International Migration, Immobility and Development*. Oxford: Berg, 1-19.

Hannabuss, S. (1996). Research interviews. *New Library World*. Vol. 97, No. 1129: 22 – 30.

Hantrais, L. (2007). Contextualization in Cross-National Comparative Research. In *Cross-National Research Methodology and Practice,* (Eds, Hantrais, L. & Mangen, S.) pp. 3-18.

Harvey, M. (1997). Dual-Career Expatriates: Expectations, Adjustment and Satisfaction with International Relocation. *Journal of International Business Studies*, 28, 627-658.

Hauser, P.M. (1974). The measurement of labour utilization. *Malayan Economic Review*, 19, 1-17.

Heaton, T.B., Clifford, W.B. & Fuguitt, G.V. (1981). Temporal shifts in the determinants of young and elderly migration in nonmetropolitan areas. *Social Forces*, 60, 41-60.

Herman, E. (2006). Migration as a Family Business: The Role of Personal Networks in the Mobility Phase of Migration, *International Migration*, 44:4, 191–230.

Higgins, M.C. (2001). Changing careers: the effects of social context. *Journal of Organizational Behavior*, 22, 595-618.

Hippler, T. (2000). European assignments: international or quasi-domestic? *Journal of European Industrial Training*, 24, 491-504.

Hochschild, A. R. (1997). *The time bind: When work becomes home and home becomes work*. New York: Metropolitan Books

Hofstede, G. (2001). *Culture's consequences: comparing values, behaviors, institutions and organizations across nations*. Second Edition, Thousand Oaks CA: Sage.

Hogg, M.A. and Terry, D.J. (2000). "Social identity and self-categorization processes in organizational contexts", *Academy of Management Review*, Vol. 25 No. 1, pp. 121-40

Holstein, J.A. & Gubrium, J.F. (1995). *The active interview*. Thousand Oaks, CA: Sage.

Home Office, (2009). Accession Monitoring Report A8 Countries, May 2004-March 2009 Available: http://webarchive.nationalarchives.gov.uk/20100422120657 /http://www.ukba.homeoffice.gov.uk/sitecontent/documents/aboutus/reports/accession_monitoring_report/report-19/may04-mar09?view=Binary [Accessed 9 Oct, 2015]

Howe N., Jackson R., Strauss R., Nakashima K. (2004). *Projecting Immigration: A Survey of the Current State of Practice and Theory*. Working Paper 2004-32, Center for Retirement Research at Boston College.

Hughes, E.C. (1997). Careers. *Qualitative Sociology*, 20, 389-397.

Hughes, G.A. & McCormick, B. (1985). Migration intentions in the UK. *The Economic Journal*, 95, 113-123.

Hugo, G. (1994). *Migration and the Family*. Vienna: United Nations Occasional Papers Series for the International Year of the Family, No. 12.

ILO (1998). Resolution concerning the measurement of underemployment and inadequate employment situations. Available http://www.ilo.org/public/english/bureau /stat/download/res/underemp.pdf [Accessed 12 July 2008]

Inkson, K., Arthur, M.B., Pringle, J. and Barry, S. (1997). Expatriate assignment versus overseas experience, *Journal of World Business*, 32:4, 351-368

Inkson, K. & Myers, B.A. (2003). "The big OE": self-directed travel and career development, *Career Development International*, 8:4, pp.170 - 181

Iredale, R. (2001). The Migration of Professionals: Theories and Typologies. *International Migration*, 39, 7-26.

Janssens, M. (1995). "Intercultural Interaction: A Burden on International Managers?," *Journal of Organizational Behavior*,16:2,155-167

Jepsen, D.A. & Choudhuri, E. (2001). Stability and change in 25-year occupational career patterns. *Career Development Quarterly*, 50, 3-19.

Johnson, P. and Harris, D. (2002). 'Qualitative and Quantitative Issues in Research Design' In Partington, D. (Ed) *Essential Skills for Management Research*, London: Sage, pp. 99-116.

Johnson, W.R. (1978). A theory of job shopping. *Quarterly Journal of Economics*, 92, 261-277.

Johnston, R., Sirkeci, I., Khattab, N., & Modood, T. (2010). Ethno-religious categories and measuring occupational attainment in relation to education in England and Wales: a multilevel analysis. *Environment and planning. A*, 42(3), 578.

Jokinen, T., Brewster, C. and Suutari, V. (2008). Career capital during international work experiences: contrasting self-initiated expatriate experiences and assigned expatriation, *The International Journal of Human Resource Management*, 19:6, 979-98.

Jovanovic, B. (1979). Job matching and the theory of turnover. *Journal of Political Economy*, 87, 972-990.

Kazlauskiene, A. & Rinkevicius, L. (2006). Lithuanian "Brain Drain" Causes: Push and Pull Factors. *Engineering Economics*, 1, 27-37.

Khapova, S. N., Arthur, M. B., Wilderom, C. P. M. & Svensson, J. S. (2007). Professional identity as the key to career change intention. *Career Development International*, 12 (7): 584-595.

Khapova, S.N., Vinkenburg, C.J. & Arnold, J., (2009). Careers research in Europe: Identity and contribution. *Journal of Occupational and Organizational Psychology*, 82(4), pp.709-719.

Khattab, N., Johnston, R., Modood, T., & Sirkeci, I. (2011). Economic activity in the South-Asian population in Britain: the impact of ethnicity, religion, and class. *Ethnic and Racial Studies*, 34(9), 1466-1481.

Kiker, B.F., Santos, M.C. & De Oliveira, M.M., (1997). Overeducation and Undereducation: Evidence for Portugal. *Economics of Education Review*, 16, 111-125.

King, N. (1998). Template analysis. In G. Symon & C. Cassell (Eds.), *Qualitative methods and analysis in organizational research: A practical guide* (pp. 118–134). London: Sage.

King, R. (2002). Towards a new map of European migration. *International Journal of Population Geography*, 8, 89-106.

King, Z., Burke, S. & Pemberton, J. (2005). The 'bounded' career: An empirical study of human capital, career mobility and employment outcomes in a mediated labour market. *Human Relations*, 58, 981-1007.

Kler, P. (2006). Graduate Overeducation and its Effects among Recently Arrived Immigrants to Australia: A Longitudinal Survey. *International Migration*, 44, 93-128.

Korczynski, M. (2005). Skills in service work: an overview. *Human Resource Management Journal*, 15:2, 3-14.

Koser, K. & Salt, J. (1997). The geography of highly skilled international migration. *International Journal of Population Geography*, 3, 285-303.

Kosic, A. (2002). Acculturation attitudes, need for cognitive closure, and adaptation of immigrants. *Journal of Social Psychology*, 142, 179–201.

Kulkarni, M., Lengnick-Hall, M.L. & Valk, R. (2010). Employee perceptions of repatriation in an emerging economy: The Indian experience *Human Resource Management*, 49:3, 531–548

Kvale, S. (1996). *Interviews: An Introduction to Qualitative Research Interviewing*. London: Sage Publications.

Lee, C.H. (2005). A study of underemployment among self-initiated expatriates. *Journal of World Business*, 40, 172-187.

Lee, R.M. (1993). *Doing Research on Sensitive Topics*. London: Sage

Lee, E.S. (1966). A Theory of Migration. *Demography*, 3, 47-57.

Lee, R.M. & Fielding, N.G. (1995). Users' Experiences of Qualitative Data Analysis Software. In Kelle, U. (Ed) *Computer-Aided Qualitative Data Analysis: Theory, Methods and Practice,* Sage, Thousand Oaks, CA, 29-40.

Lewins, A. & Silver, C. (2007). *Using Software for Qualitative Data Analysis: A step-by- step Guide*. Thousand Oaks, CA: Sage.

Lianos, T.P. (2007). Brain Drain and Brain Loss: Immigrants to Greece. *Journal of Ethnic and Migration Studies*, 33, 129-140.

Lichtenstein, B., & Mendenhall, M. (2002). Non-linearity and Response-Ability: Emergent order in 21st century careers. *Human Relations*, 55:1, 5-32

Lincoln, Y. S., & Guba, E. G. (1985). Naturalistic inquiry. Beverly Hills, CA: Sage

Linsley, I. (2005). *Cases of Overeducation in the Australian Labour Market*. Research Paper Number 940, Department of Economics, the University of Melbourne

Liversage, A. (2009). Finding a Path: Investigating the Labour Market Trajectories of High-Skilled Immigrants in Denmark. *Journal of Ethnic and Migration Studies*, 35, 203-226.

Lonkila, M. (1995). Grounded Theory as an Emerging Paradigm for Computer-assisted Qualitative Data Analysis. In Kelle, U. (Ed) *Computer-Aided Qualitative Data Analysis: Theory, Methods and Practice,* Sage, Thousand Oaks, CA, 41-51.

Louis, M.R. (1980). Career Transitions: Varieties and Commonalities. *Academy of Management Review*, 5, 329-340.

MacMillan, K. (2005). More than just coding? Evaluating CAQDAS in a discourse analysis of news texts. Available online at: http://www.qualitative-research.net/fqs- texte/3-05/05-3-25-e.htm [Accessed June 4, 2008]

Macmillan, K. & Koening, T. (2004) The Wow Factor: Preconceptions and Expectations for Data Analysis Software in Qualitative Research. *Social Science Computer Review*, 22, 179-186.

Madsen, K.D. & T. Van Naerssen (2003). Migration, identity and belonging, *Journal of Borderlands Studies* 18(1): 61-75.

Mahroum, S. (2000). Highly Skilled Globetrotters: Mapping the International Migration of Human Capital. *R & D Management,* 30, 23-32.

Marshall, C. & Rossman, G. B. (2006). *Designing Qualitative Research*, 4th edition, Thousand Oaks: Sage.

Martel, Y. (2003). *Life of Pi*, Edinburgh, Canon Gate.

Martin, P. L., (1994). Immigration and Integration: Challenges for the 1990s, *Social Contract*, 177-181

Massey, D.S. (1990). "Social Structure, Household Strategies, and the Cumulative Causation of Migration," *Population Index*, 56, 1-26.

Massey, D.S., Arango J., Hugo, G., Kouaouci, A. Pellegrino, A. and Taylor, J.E. (1993). "Theories of International Migration: A Review and Appraisal," *Population and Development Review*, 19, 431-466

Massey, D.S., Arango, J., Hugo, G., Kouaouci, A., Pellegrino, A. and Taylor, J.E. (1998). *Worlds in Motion: Understanding International Migration at the End of Millennium*, Oxford, Oxford University Press.

Massey, D.S., & Sanchez M., (2010). *Brokered Boundaries: Creating Immigrant Identity in Anti-Immigrant Times*, New York, Russell Sage Foundation

Mayrhofer, W. & Schneidhofer, T. M. (2009). The lay of the land: European career research and its future *Journal of Occupational and Organizational Psychology,* 82:4, 721–737.

Mayrhofer, W., Sparrow, P. R., & Zimmermann, A. (2008). Modern forms of international working. In M. Dickmann, C. Brewster, & P. R. Sparrow (Eds.), International human resource management: Contemporary issues in Europe (pp. 219–239). London: Routledge.

McCall, G. J., and J. L. Simmons (1978). *Identities and Interactions: An Examination of Human Association in Everyday Life*. New York: Free Press.

McCall, G. (2003). The me and the not-me: Positive and negative poles of identity. In P. J. Burke, T. J. Owens, R. T. Serpe, & P. A. Thoits (Eds.), *Advances in identity theory and research* (pp. 11-25). New York: Plenum

McKay, S. & Winkelmann-Gleed, A. (2005). *Migrant workers in the East of England Project Report*. London Metropolitan University.

McKenzie DJ, & Mistiaen J. (2009). Surveying migrant households: a comparison of census-based, snowball and intercept point surveys. *Journal of the Royal Statistical Society*: Series A (Statistics in Society), 172,339–360

Mendenhall, M. E., Beaty, D., & Oddou, G.R. (1993). Where have all the theorists gone? *International Journal of Management, 10, 146-153.*

Mendenhall, M.E., Osland, J.S., Bird, A., Oddou, G.R., Maznevski, M.L. (2008). *Global leadership: research, practice, and development*. Routledge, London

Miles, M. (1979). Qualitative data as an attractive nuisance: The problem of analysis. *Administrative Science Quarterly.* 24. 590-601.

Miles, M.B. & Huberman, A.M. (1994) *Qualitative data analysis: an expanded sourcebook*. Thousand Oaks, CA: Sage.

Miller, K., Haskell, C., Thatcher, A. (2002). The relationship between intention to emigrate and organisational commitment, *South African Journal of Psychology,* 32, 3, 16-20

Musson, G. (1998). Life histories. In C. Cassell (Ed.), *Qualitative Methods and Analysis in Organizational Research* (pp. 10-27). London: Sage.

Myrdal, G. (1957). *Economic Theory and Underdeveloped Regions*, London, Gerald Duckworth.

Newman, K. (1999). *Falling from grace: Downward mobility in the age of affluence*. Berkeley, CA: University of California Press.

Nicholson, N. (1984). A theory of work role transitions. *Administrative Science Quarterly*, 29, 172-191.

Nicholson, N. (1990). The transition cycle: causes, outcomes, processes and forms. In S. Fisher & C. L. Cooper (Eds.), *On the move: The psychological effects of change and transition* (pp.83–108). Chichester: Wiley

Nicholson, N. & West, M. (1988). *Managerial job change: men and women in transition*. Cambridge: Cambridge University Press.

Nicholson, N. and West, M. (1989). Transitions, work histories and careers. In M. B. Arthur, D. T. Hall and B. S. Lawrence (eds), *Handbook of Career Theory*. Cambridge: Cambridge University Press, pp. 181-201

Nielsen, Ch. P. (2007). *Immigrant Overeducation: Evidence from Denmark,* World Bank Policy Research Working Paper 4234.

Noon, M. & Blyton, P. (1997). *The Realities of Work.* Basingstoke, Macmillan.

Oakley, A. (1981). Interviewing women: a contradiction in terms. In: H. Roberts, Editor, *Doing Feminist Research*, Routledge, London, pp. 31-61

Ochs, E. (1979). Transcription as theory. In, E. Ochs & B. Schieffelin. (Eds) *Developmental pragmatics.* New York. Academic, Press, pp. 43–72.

OECD (2006). *International Migration Outlook*, Annual Report 2006, OECD, Paris.

Oliver, P. (2000). *Employment for professional migrants to New Zealand - barriers and opportunities*, a report prepared for Work and Income New Zealand

Owens, T.J. (2003). Self and Identity. In J. DeLamater (Ed) *Handbook of Social Psychology, Vol. 5,* Kluwer, New York, pp. 205-232.

Palloni, A., Massey, D. S., Ceballos, M., Espinosa, K. E. and Spittel. M. (2001). "Social Capital and International Migration: A Test Using Information on Family Networks." *American Journal of Sociology* 106:1262-98.

Palthe, J. (2004). The relative importance of antecedents to cross-cultural adjustment: Implications for managing a global workforce. *International Journal of Intercultural Relations*, 28, 37-59.

Patrinos, H.A. (1997). Overeducation in Greece. *International Review of Education*, 43, 203-223.

Patton, M. Q. (1990). *Qualitative research methods and evaluation* (3rd ed.).Thousand Oaks, CA: Sage.

Patton, M.Q., (2002). *Qualitative Research and Evaluation Methods*, Thousand Oaks CA, Sage Publications

Peltokorpi, V. (2007). Intercultural communication patterns and tactics: Nordic expatriates in Japan. *International Business Review*, 16, 68-82.

Peltokorpi, V., & Froese, F.J. (2009). Organizational expatriates and self-initiated expatriates: Who adjusts better to work and life in Japan? *International Journal of Human Resource Management,* 20(5), 1095-1111.

Peltonen, T. (2001). *New forms of international work: an international survey study, Results of the Finnish Survey.* University of Oulu (in association with Cranfield Management School), Finland.

Pemberton, S. (2008). Supporting Economic Migrants in the North West of England Implications for Economic and Social Policy. *Public Policy and Administration*, 23, 81-100.

Penninx, R., Spencer, D. & Hear, N.V. (2008). *Migration and Integration in Europe: The State of Research*. ESRC Centre on Migration, Policy and Society (COMPAS), Oxford, University of Oxford.

Phinney, J. S. (1990). Ethnic identity in adolescents and adults: Review of research. *Psychological Bulletin*, 108, 499-514.

Piore, M.J. (1979). *Birds of passage: migrant labor and industrial societies*. Cambridge. Cambridge University Press.

Piracha, M. and R. Vickerman (2002). "Immigration, labour mobility and EU enlargement", Department of Economics, University of Kent

Portes, A. & Borocz, J. (1989). Contemporary Immigration: Theoretical Perspectives on Its Determinants and Modes Of Incorporation. *International Migration Review*, 23, 606-630.

Remennick, L. (1999). Women with a Russian accent in Israel: On the gender aspects of migration. *European Journal of Women's Studies* 6 (4): 441-461

Remenyi, D., Williams, B., Money, A., and Swartz, E. (1998). *Doing research in business and management: an introduction to process and method*. London: Sage.

Reyneri, E. (2004). Education and the Occupational Pathways of Migrants in Italy. *Journal of Ethnic and Migration Studies*, 30:6, 1145-1162.

Richardson, J. (2003). *Experiencing expatriation: A study of expatriate academics*. Unpublished Doctor of Philosophy thesis, University of Otago, Dunedin.

Richardson, J. (2006). Self directed expatriation: family matters, *Personnel Review*, 35:4, 469-86.

Robinson, V. (2002). Migrant workers in the UK. *Labour market trends*, September, 2002, 467-476

Robinson, V. & Carey, M. (2000). Peopling skilled international migration: Indian doctors in the U.K. *International Migration*, 38, 89-108.

Robst, J. (1995). Career mobility, job match, and overeducation. *Eastern Economics Journal*, 21:4, 539-550.

Rooth, D. & Ekberg, J. (2006). Occupational Mobility for Immigrants in Sweden. *International Migration*, 44, 57-77.

Rubb, S. (2003). Overeducation: a short or long run phenomenon for individuals? *Economics of Education Review*, 22, 389-394.

Salt, J. & Singleton, A. (1995). Analysis and Forecasting of International Migration by Major Groups. Report prepared on behalf of Eurostat. London: Migration Research Unit, University College of London.

Salt, John. 1997. International movements of the highly skilled. International Migration Unit Occasional Paper no. 3. Paris: OECD

Sargent, L.D. (2003). Effects of a downward status transition on perceptions of career success, role performance and job identification. *Australian Journal of Psychology,* 55, 114-120.

Savickas, M.L. (2002). Reinvigorating the Study of Careers. *Journal of Vocational Behavior*, 61, 381-385.

Sayad, A. (2004). *The Suffering of the Immigrant*. Cambridge: Polity Press.

Schein, E. H. (1996). Career anchors revisited: implications for career development in the 21st century. Academy of Management Executive, 10:4, 80–88.

Schmitter Heisler, B. (2000) "The Sociology of Immigration. From Assimilation to Segmented Integration, from the American Experience to the Global Era" In Bretell, C. and J. F. Hollifield (Eds) *Migration Theory. Talking across Disciplines* New York: Routledge, 77-96

Schmitz, P. G. (1994). Acculturation and adaptation processes among immigrants in Germany. In: M. Bouvy, F. J. R. Van de Vijver, P. Boski, & P. Schmitz (Eds.), *Journeys into cross-cultural psychology: Selected papers from the Eleventh International Conference of the International Association for Cross-Cultural Psychology* (pp. 142-157). Lisse, the Netherlands: Swets & Zeitlinger.

Schneider, C. & Holman, D. (2005). *A profile of migrant workers in the Breckland area, Keystone Development Trust.* Available: http://www.keystonetrust.org.uk/ communities/index.php?page=22 [Accessed 29 June 2007]

Schneider, C. & Holman, D. (2009). Longitudinal Study of Migrant Workers in the East of England, Interim Report, East of England Development Agency, European Social Fund

Schuster, A., Desiderio, M. V., & Urso, G. (2013). Recognition of Qualifications and Competencies of Migrants. Brussels: International Organization for Migration Available: http://publications.iom.int/bookstore/free/Recognition_Qualifications _CompetencesofMigrants.pdf [Accessed 8 October 2015]

Schwandt, T.A. (1997). *Qualitative Inquiry: A Dictionary of Terms.* Thousand Oaks, CA: Sage.

Scott, S. (2006). The Social Morphology of Skilled Migration: The Case of the British Middle Class in Paris. *Journal of Ethnic and Migration Studies*, 32, 1105-1129.

Seidel, J. & Kelle, U. (1995). Different Functions of Coding in the Analysis of Data. In Kelle, U. (Ed) *Computer-Aided Qualitative Data Analysis: Theory, Methods and Practice,* Sage, Thousand Oaks, CA, pp. 29-40.

Seidman, I. (2006). *Interviewing as qualitative research: A guide for researchers in education and the social sciences.* New York: Teachers College Press

Selmer, J. (1998). Expatriation: corporate policy, personal intentions and international adjustment. *The International Journal of Human Resource Management*, 9, 996-1007.

Shah, C. & Long, M. G. (2009). Labour mobility and mutual recognition of skills and qualifications: The European Union and Australia/New Zealand, in Rupert Maclean and David N. Wilson (Eds). *International Handbook of Education for the Changing World of Work: Bridging Academic and Vocational Learning*, Springer Science+Business Media B.V., Germany, pp. 2935-2951.

Shaw, I. and Gould, N. (eds) (2001). Qualitative Research in Social Work: Method and Context. Newbury Park, CA: Sage

Shay, J.P. & Baack, S.A. (2004). Expatriate assignment, adjustment, and effectiveness: An empirical examination of the big picture. *Journal of International Business Studies*, 35, 216-232.

Shih, J. (2002). ' " ... Yeah, I Could Hire this One, But I Know it's Going to be a Problem": How Race, Nativity and Gender Affect Employer' Perceptions of the Manageability of Job-seekers', *Ethnic and Racial Studies* 25(1): 99–119

Sicherman, N. (1991). 'Overeducation' in the labor market. *Journal of Labor Economics*, 9:2, 101-122.

Silverman, D. (2005). *Doing Qualitative Research: A Practical Handbook.* Thousand Oaks, CA: Sage.

Simic, M. (2002). Volume of underemployment and overemployment in the UK (Part 1). *Labour Market trends*, 399-414.

Sirkeci, I. (2009). Transnational mobility and conflict. *Migration Letters*, 6(1), 3-14.

Sirkeci, I., Acik, N., & Saunders, B. (2014). Discriminatory labour market experiences of A8 national high skilled workers in the UK. *Border Crossing: Transnational Working Papers*, 2014(1402), 17-31.

Skeldon, R. (2005). Globalization, Skilled Migration and Poverty Alleviation: Brain Drains in Context. *Development Research Centre on Migration, Globalisation and Poverty Working Paper T15,* DFID/ University of Sussex

Slay, H.S. (2006). *The Influence of Career Identity and Social Networks on Career Transition Magnitude.* Unpublished Doctor of Philosophy thesis. University of Maryland. Maryland

Sloane, P.J., Battu, H. & Seaman, P.T. (1999). Overeducation, undereducation and the British labour market. *Applied Economics*, 31, 1437-1453.

Smith, H.L. (1986). Overeducation and Underemployment: An Agnostic Review. *Sociology of Education*, 59, 85-99.

Solimano A. (2006). The international mobility of talent and its impact on global development. Discussion Paper No 2006/08. Geneva: UNU-WIDER.

Speare, A., Kobrin, F. & Kingkade, W. (1982). The influence of socio-economic bonds and satisfaction on interstate migration. *Social Forces*, 61, 551-574.

Spencer, S., Ruhs, M., Anderson, B. and Rogaly, B. (2007). Migrants' lives beyond the workplace. Joseph Rowntree Foundation, York

Sretenova, N. (2003). *Scientific Mobility and Brain Drain Issues in the Context of Structural Reforms of Research and Development and the Higher Education Sector in Bulgaria.* University of Leeds, CSLPE Research Report 2.

Stahl, G.K. & Caligiuri, P. (2005). The Effectiveness of Expatriate Coping Strategies: The Moderating Role of Cultural Distance, Position Level, and Time on the International Assignment. *Journal of Applied Psychology*, 90, 603-615.

Staller, K.M. (2002). Musings of a Skeptical Software Junkie and the Hyper Research™ Fix. *Qualitative Social Work*, 1, 473-487.

Stark, O. (1984). Migration decision making: A review article. *Journal of Development Economics*, 14, 251-259.

Stenning A, Champion T, Conway C, Coombes M, Dawley S, Dixon L, Raybould S, Richardson R. (2006). *Assessing the Local and Regional Impacts of International Migration.* ODPM: London

Stephens, G. K. (1994). Crossing internal career boundaries: The state of research on subjective career transitions. J*ournal of Management, 20*, 479–501.

Stets, J.E. & Burke, P.J. (2003). A Sociological Approach to Self and Identity. In, In, M. Leary, and J. Tangney, (Eds) Handbook *of Self and Identity.* Guilford Press, New York, pp. 128-152.

Strauss, A., & Corbin, J. (1990). *Basics of qualitative research: Grounded theory procedures and techniques.* Newbury Park, CA: Sage Publications, Inc.

Stryker, S. & Burke, P.J. (2000). The Past, Present, and Future of an Identity Theory. *Social Psychology Quarterly*, 63, 284-297.

Sullivan, S.E. (1999). The changing nature of careers: a review and research agenda. *Journal of Management*, 25:3, 457-484.

Sullivan, S.E. & Baruch, Y. (2009). Advances in Career Theory and Research: A Critical Review and Agenda for Future Exploration. *Journal of Management*, 35, 1542-1571.

Sullivan, T.A. (1978). *Marginal workers, marginal jobs: The underutilization of American workers*. Austin, University of Texas Press.

Suutari, V. & Brewster, C. (2000). Making their own way: international experience through self-initiated foreign assignments. *Journal of World Business*, 35, 417-436.

Takeuchi, R., Yun, S., & Russell, J. E. A. (2002). Antecedents and consequences of the perceived adjustment of Japanese expatriates in the USA. *International Journal of Human Resource Management*, 13(8): 1224-1244.

Tassinopoulos A., & Werner H. (1999). 'To Move or Not to move – Migration of Labour in the European Union.' *IAB Labour Market Research Topics 35*.

Taylor, E.J. (1999). The New Economics of Labour Migration and the Role of Remittances in the Migration Process. *International Migration*, 37, 63-88.

Temple, B. & Young, A. (2004). Qualitative Research and Translation Dilemmas. *Qualitative Research*, 4, 161–178.

Thomas, D. C., and Inkson, K. (2007). Careers across cultures. In H. Gunz and M. Peiperl (eds). *Handbook of Career Studies* pp. 451-470. Thousand Oaks, CA: Sage.

Thomas, D.C., Lazarova, M.B. & Inkson, K. (2005). Global careers: New phenomenon or new perspectives? *Journal of World Business*, 40, 340-347.

Thompson, J.A. & Van, A.H. (2002). Commitment Shift during Organizational Upheaval: Physicians' Transitions from Private Practitioner to Employee. *Journal of Vocational Behavior*, 60, 382-404.

Timotijevic, L., & Breakwell, G. M. (2000). Migration and threat to identity. *Journal of Community & Applied Social Psychology*, 10, 355-372

Todaro, M. (1980). Internal Migration in Developing Countries: A Survey In R. A. Easterlin, (ed) *Population and Economic Change in Developing Countries*. Chicago. University of Chicago Press, pp. 361 - 402

Todisco, E., Brandi, M.C. & Tattolo, G. (2003). Skilled migration: a theoretical framework and the case of foreign researchers in Italy. *FULGOR*, 1, 115-130.

Tracy, S. J., & Trethewey, A. (2005). Fracturing the real-self↔fake-self dichotomy: Moving toward "crystallized" organizational discourses and identities. *Communication Theory*, 15, 168-195

Trevena, P. (2006). The Polish "Intelligentsia" in London: a case study of young graduates working in the secondary sector. Paper presented at CRONEM seminar, 27 March 2006

Trevena, P. (2009). "New" Polish migration to the UK: a synthesis of existing evidence, Centre for Population Change Working Papers No 3/2009

Trevena, P. (2010). *The Polish "Intelligentsia" in London: A Case Study of Young Graduates Working in the Secondary Sector* .Unpublished Doctor of Philosophy thesis, Polish Academy of Sciences, Warsaw.

Tsang, E. W. K. (1998). Mind Your Identity When Conducting Cross-National Research. *Organization Studies*, 19, 511–515.

Tsang, M.C., Rumberger, R.W. & Levin, H.M. (1991). The Impact of Surplus Schooling on Worker Productivity. *Industrial Relations*, 30, 209-228.

UNFPA (2005). Linking Population, Poverty and Development Migration: A World on the Move, Available: http://www.unfpa.org/pds/migration.html [Accessed 21 March 2011]

van Gennep, A. (1960). *The Rites of Passage*. Chicago: University of Chicago Press.

Van Oudenhoven, J. P., & Eisses, A.-M. (1998). Integration and assimilation of Moroccan immigrants in Israel and the Netherlands. *International Journal of Intercultural Relations*, 22, 293 – 307.

Van Vianen, A.E.M. et al. (2004). Fitting in: Surface- and deep-level cultural differences and expatriates' adjustment. *Academy of Management Journal*, 47, 697-709.

Vandenbrande, T., Coppin, L., Van der Hallen, P., Ester, P., Fouarge, D., Fasang, A., Geerdes, S. and Schömann, K. (2006). *Mobility in Europe*, Luxembourg: Office for Official Publications of the European Communities.

Vertovec, S. (2002). *Transnational Networks and Skilled Labour Migration*. Oxford: Economic and Social Research Council/University of Oxford.

Waddington, S. (2007). *Routes to integration and inclusion; new approaches to enable refugee and migrant workers to progress in the labour market*. Leicester. NIACE

Waldinger, R., Bozorgmehr, M., Lim, N., & Finkel, L. (1998). *In search of the glass ceiling: the career trajectories of migrant and native-born engineers*. The Lewis Center for Regional Policy Studies, Working Paper #28, Los Angeles, CA.

Wales Rural Observatory (2006). *Scoping Study on Eastern and Central European Migrant Workers in Wales*. Cardiff: Cardiff University/University of Wales

Wallace, C. (1998). *Migration Potential in Central and Eastern Europe*, International Organization for Migration (IOM), Geneva.

Wallerstein, I. (1974). *The Modern World System 1: Capitalist Agriculture and the Origins of the European World-economy in the Sixteenth Century*. New York. Academic Press.

Ward, C., & Kennedy, A. (1994). Acculturation strategies, psychological adjustment, and sociocultural competence during cross-cultural transitions. International Journal of Intercultural Relations, 18, 329–343.

Warnes, A.M. & Williams, A. (2006). Older Migrants in Europe: A New Focus for Migration Studies. *Journal of Ethnic and Migration Studies*, 32, 1257-1281.

Watson, I. (1996). *Opening the Glass Door: Overseas-born Managers in Australia*. South Melbourne: BIMPR and ACIRRT.

Webb, A. and Wright, P. (1996). The expatriate experience: implications for career success, *Career Development International*, Vol. 8 No. 3, pp. 38-44.

Weick, K. E. (1995). Sensemaking in organizations. Thousand Oaks, CA: Sage

Weick, K. E. (1996). Enactment and the boundaryless career: Organizing as we work. In M. B. Arthur, & D. M. Rousseau (Eds.), *The boundaryless career: A new employment principle for a new organizational era* (pp. 40–57). New York: Oxford University Press.

Weishaar, H.B. (2008). 'Consequences of international migration: A qualitative study on stress among Polish migrant workers in Scotland', *Public Health* 122: 1250–1256

Weitzman, E.A. & Miles, B. (1995). *Computer programs for qualitative data analysis: a software sourcebook*. Thousand Oaks, CA: Sage.

Welch, C. & Piekkari, R. (2006). Crossing language boundaries: Qualitative interviewing in international business. *Management International Review*, 46, 417–437.

Wolpert, J. (1965). Behavioral aspects of the decision to migrate. *Papers of the Regional Science Association*, 15, 159-169.

Zaronaite, D. and Tirzite, A. (2006). *The Dynamics of Migrant Labour in South Lincolnshire*, East Midlands Development Agency.

Zikic J., Novicevic M.M., Harvey M., & Breland, J. (2006). Repatriate career exploration: a path to career growth and success. *Career Development International*, 11, 633-649.

Zikic, J., Bonache, J. & Cerdin, J.-L. (2010). Crossing national boundaries: A typology of qualified immigrants' career orientations. *Journal of Organizational Behavior*, 31, 667-686.

Zimmermann, A., Holman, D. & Sparrow, P. (2003). "Unravelling Adjustment Mechanisms: Adjustment of German Expatriates to Intercultural Interactions, Work and Living Conditions in the People's Republic of China", *International Journal of Cross Cultural Management*, 3:1, 45- 66.

Zulauf, M. (1999). Cross national qualitative research: accommodating ideals and reality. *International Journal of Social Research Methodology*, 2:2, 159- 169.

Saunders

Index

www.ingramcontent.com/pod-product-compliance
Lightning Source LLC
Chambersburg PA
CBHW021942220326
41599CB00013BA/1653